PRAISE FOR *FLEXIE*

D1462286

'An excellent "how to do it" book that helps employers think through their options for flexible working in the new world of work. This is a very well written and extremely timely book and will support the HR community in thinking through how we work in the future.'
Professor Sir Cary Cooper, Alliance Manchester Business School, University of Manchester

'From formulating a strategy to launching and embedding flexible working practices across the organization, this book is the perfect companion to this potentially daunting task. Part One of the book sets out the rich evidential basis for flexible working as a driver of organizational performance and its impact on the bottom line. Part Two provides a step-by-step approach to ensuring that a move towards flexible working is not only successful from day one but also sustainable in the longer term. Packed with case studies, practical examples and useful templates, this book is a must-read for forward-looking businesses of all sizes.'
Karen Teago, CEO and Principal Solicitor, Your Employment Settlement Service

'An accessible and well-reasoned contribution to thinking about and understanding flexible work. It not only makes a clear case for the benefits of organizations taking a flexible approach to work, but also offers clear and easily implementable interventions to overcome some of the most commonly faced barriers. It does this while also calling out, with gusto, those areas where myth, bluster or lazy assumptions have dominated the debate.'
David D'Souza, Membership Director, CIPD

'This book is a must-read for any HR practitioner or business leader who wants to create a more flexible future for their organization. As well as providing the evidence to build the business case, it delivers a complete and practical guide to every step that you need to take along the way. Gemma Dale provides us with compelling reasons to rethink how and where we work.'
Tim Scott, People Director, Fletchers Solicitors

'If you are an HR professional or a line manager, this comprehensive book will take you on a learning journey, giving you both an introductory blast into what flexible working means through to embedding it into your organization's strategy and culture. It uniquely does the horizon scanning for you as you consider the future and how flexible working can support other big workplace agendas such as wellbeing, attracting talent and inclusion. Myths are dispelled, barriers explored and toolkits included to help to create a flexible working culture and embed flexible working practices. It's a must read. Five stars from me!'

Daphne Doody-Green, Head of CIPD Northern England

'Punchy, comprehensive and thorough, this book covers everything you need to know about this vital subject. If you're still in any doubt that flexible working should be part of our present and future, you'll be left with a clear sense that this is the right thing to do and be equipped with all the information, perspectives and tools needed to make it happen. You can't afford to be without this book.'

Neil Usher, Chief Partnerships Officer, GoSpace AI, and author of _The Elemental Workplace_

Flexible Working

How to implement flexibility in the workplace to improve employee and business performance

Gemma Dale

KoganPage

Publisher's note

Every possible effort has been made to ensure that the information contained in this book is accurate at the time of going to press, and the publishers and author cannot accept responsibility for any errors or omissions, however caused. No responsibility for loss or damage occasioned to any person acting, or refraining from action, as a result of the material in this publication can be accepted by the editor, the publisher or the author.

First published in Great Britain and the United States in 2021 by Kogan Page Limited

Apart from any fair dealing for the purposes of research or private study, or criticism or review, as permitted under the Copyright, Designs and Patents Act 1988, this publication may only be reproduced, stored or transmitted, in any form or by any means, with the prior permission in writing of the publishers, or in the case of reprographic reproduction in accordance with the terms and licences issued by the CLA. Enquiries concerning reproduction outside these terms should be sent to the publishers at the undermentioned addresses:

2nd Floor, 45 Gee Street	122 W 27th St, 10th Floor	4737/23 Ansari Road
London	New York, NY 10001	Daryaganj
EC1V 3RS	USA	New Delhi 110002
United Kingdom		India
www.koganpage.com		

Kogan Page books are printed on paper from sustainable forests.

© Gemma Dale, 2021

The right of Gemma Dale to be identified as the author of this work has been asserted by her in accordance with the Copyright, Designs and Patents Act 1988.

ISBNs

Hardback	978 1 78966 591 8
Paperback	978 1 78966 589 5
Ebook	978 1 78966 590 1

British Library Cataloguing-in-Publication Data

A CIP record for this book is available from the British Library.

Library of Congress Cataloging-in-Publication Data

Names: Dale, Gemma, author.
Title: Flexible working : how to implement flexibility in the workplace to
   improve employee and business performance / Gemma Dale.
Description: London, United Kingdom ; New York, NY : Kogan Page, 2021.
   Includes bibliographical references and index.
Identifiers: LCCN 2020041863 (print) | LCCN 2020041864 (ebook) | ISBN
   9781789665895 (paperback) | ISBN 9781789665918 (hardback) | ISBN
   9781789665901 (ebook)
Subjects: LCSH: Flexible work arrangements. | Flextime. | Organizational
   change.
Classification: LCC HD5109 .D35 2021 (print) | LCC HD5109 (ebook) | DDC
   658.3/123—dc23
LC record available at https://lccn.loc.gov/2020041863
LC ebook record available at https://lccn.loc.gov/2020041864

Typeset by Hong Kong FIVE Workshop, Hong Kong
Print production managed by Jellyfish
Printed and bound by CPI Group (UK) Ltd, Croydon CR0 4YY

CONTENTS

ACKNOWLEDGEMENTS

This book could not have been written without the constant support of my partner Tim. Many thanks are due to him for services to grammar and punctuation.

I am particularly indebted to the organizations and academics whose research, experiences and survey data is discussed throughout this book. Thank you for your insights, without which this book would not have been possible.

Thanks are also due to the team at Kogan Page for providing me with the opportunity to write about this subject.

Introduction

Why flexible working and why now?

Since the Industrial Revolution, a great deal of the work that many of us undertake has continued to be done in a very similar way and within a similar structure, both of which will be familiar to most employees today. For a significant proportion of the current workforce, our daily work involves travelling to a particular location where we will find others undertaking their own work for the same organization. The work itself typically takes place between Monday and Friday (although in the not-too-distant past working Saturday too was also commonplace) and broadly between the hours of 9am and 5pm, with just a few minor variations on this theme. When the particular work activities or working hours are completed, employees travel home again. In this model, work is both an activity that we undertake as well as a place to which we go.

Although in our 24/7 culture this description is not necessarily true of all organizations or job roles, it is a model that we know well, and it is the default way of working for many employees. There are some obvious reasons why work evolved in this way. Although today many of our industries are now service-driven and technology-filled, in the recent past employees needed to travel to a particular place in order to physically undertake their work (such as working on a production line in a manufacturing plant) or to communicate with other workers face to face. Simply, for many years, the default model of work was a necessity; there was no feasible alternative. This default model not only continues to dominate, but has also proved particularly resistant to change.

In many respects, these ways of working pertain to a previous generation and previous ideas of work. This is how our parents and grandparents worked, and they did so because the nature and organization of their work demanded it. These models have, however, in recent years come under increasing pressure as the very nature of jobs, as well as how and where work can be completed, have fundamentally changed. The ideas and approaches of previous decades, indeed centuries, no longer hold true. The traditional command and control manager, providing direct supervision and telling people what to do and when to do it, equally has less and less relevance in the current world of work. In today's economy, more and more of us undertake what is often termed 'knowledge work': work that requires people to think and process information for a living, applying their specialist experiences and learning. Knowledge workers therefore do not work in a factory or on a production line, and there is no need for them to behave, or lead, as if they do.

Whilst both the possibilities and technologies within the workplace have evolved, our approaches to *how* we work have not kept pace. Many organizations still work in the old ways, acting as if the old barriers to alternatives exist. We are, perhaps, so used to the Monday to Friday, location-based, default model of work, that it is difficult to see the potential of a new way. If we choose, however, to step back for just a moment and look at both work and organizational behaviour with fresh eyes, many of the ways in which we undertake and organize much of the work that we do make little sense today for a lot of employees, their managers and their places of work.

Consider this example. Although commuting distances and start times will vary, many of us leave our homes for our place of work in the morning, each of us doing so around a similar time – the so-called rush hour. We get into our cars or onto buses, trams and trains, all of us again at the same time, for which, in terms of public transport at least, we pay a premium. For those who drive to work, we may find ourselves in heavy traffic or contending with expensive city-centre car-parking charges. These commutes create a carbon footprint, take time and add to workers' stress levels. Many people use this commuting time to undertake even more work, adding to their working day by responding to emails on the train or making calls from the car. Upon arrival at our places of work we normally sit at the same desk, engage with the same people, send emails to and sit in meetings with them. We do much of our work by using tools and technology that could be used anywhere. At the end of the working day we return to our homes, undertaking our trying journeys in reverse. The question arises: if we invented work tomorrow, is this how we would choose to organize it? Is this really the most sensible way in which to work and earn a living, in the early 21st century?

As we continue to shift towards an economy made up increasingly of knowledge workers, many people can work from anywhere or any when, as long as they have a reliable wifi connection and a laptop. Most of our communication and collaboration can be effectively undertaken online without detriment to the process. It is not just ways of working and technology that have changed. Job roles that didn't exist 20 years ago have emerged and even become commonplace: for example, until recently, marketing teams had no requirement for a social media manager or an SEO (search engine optimization) specialist. Other roles have disappeared altogether, as have major organizations and household names – some of them because they were unable to shift to meet changing cultures and customer demands.

Although the ability to work in a radically different way does not of course apply to all types of worker and job roles, it does (or certainly can) apply to a significant proportion of the working population. Problematically, however, when individuals do try to step outside of accepted workplace norms and seek to work differently, this often results in a negative impact on their career or earnings as well as poorer perceptions of them as a worker.

It is entirely possible for many professionals and occupations to work in a different way to the standard or default working week, and in particular many people can work in a much more flexible way than they do today. This flexibility can bring with it a wide range of benefits to all parties in the employment relationship.

Quite simply, we can have a *flexible working revolution*.

The Chartered Institute of Personnel and Development (CIPD) defines flexible working as: 'a type of working arrangement which gives a degree of flexibility on how long, where, when and at what times employees work' (CIPD, 2019). Many organizations have, in recent years, begun to recognize the potential of flexible working arrangements, and that adopting different approaches to how, where and when work is organized can have significant benefits for the organization itself and those people who work for it. These changes are not of course without their challenges (some of which are significant), but it is entirely possible to overcome these with commitment and action. Some of those forward-thinking organizations, already experiencing the benefits of flexibility, have shared their stories for the purposes of this book.

It has occasionally been said that flexibility is the 'new normal' and that '9 to 5' is a thing of the past, but whilst this is an appealing soundbite, it does not appear to be a lived reality for many employees today. Science fiction writer William Gibson is known for his popular – although potentially apocryphal – quote, 'The future is already here, it is just not evenly distributed.' This could perhaps also be said of flexible working.

Generally speaking, the use of flexible working appears to be increasing – but not especially quickly. A 2018 survey by XpertHR found that over half of employers said that the number of requests for flexible working they were receiving had increased over the last two years, something that respondents attributed to two factors: changing workforce demographics and more supportive working cultures (XpertHR, 2018). However, take a look beyond the headlines and top-level percentages and a much more mixed picture emerges. Whilst a range of research and surveys undertaken by both academics and industry bodies have identified multiple benefits of flexible working, research also suggests that many employees and organizations are dissatisfied with their lived experiences and outcomes (Clarke and Holdsworth, 2017).

The right to request flexible working was introduced into UK employment law several years ago, but problems inherent within the drafting of the legislation, as well as a range of other factors that we will consider in more depth throughout this book, have limited its impact. What we are currently experiencing is a spectrum of flexibility, both in general and then specifically within organizations and even specific departments and teams. From the workplace that entirely embraces flexibility as the standard way of working to the one that will only permit an occasional, minor adaption to standard working hours (and everything in between), flexible working in the UK is highly variable.

Although the trend towards more flexibility is broadly moving in the right direction, progress in many organizations is slow. The default model of work appears to be stubbornly resistant to change. Many businesses continue to ignore flexible working, treating individual flexible working requests as a nuisance and flexible working arrangements as something to be tolerated. Flexible working in this context is something that is only for the employee; the broader benefits are neither recognized nor realized, and tensions within teams can result when limited flexibility is provided.

Somewhat perversely, it seems that many organizations recognize the importance of their people and operations *being* flexible. This language conjures up ideas of agility, adaptability and responsiveness to changing demands or needs. This type of flexibility is very much a good thing from an organizational perspective. When we apply the same concept to employees, however, it often seems that little bit less desirable. Whilst many businesses want people to *be* flexible, to possess this competency, they are seemingly not as happy for them to *do* flexibility in the form of how the work is carried out.

It is not uncommon to see organizations, on their websites or within their employer brand material, espousing their support for working parents or their flexibility as an employer. Unfortunately, the employee experience in reality is often all too different to the marketing and PR rhetoric. There can be a significant gap between what is said to be done and what actually happens in practice. This has been referred to as 'flex-washing': a veneer of publicized flexibility but without real substance for much of the workforce (Timewise, 2019).

Whatever beliefs an organization may have about flexible working, the UK government broadly accepts the rationale for it, and its importance was recognized in the 2017 Taylor Review into modern working practices. This report considered the steps necessary to ensure fair and decent work for all employees and recognized the importance and benefits of flexible working to individuals and organizations. The report specifically recommended that the government needed to go further to promote genuine flexibility in the workplace, tackle some of the cultural and practical issues that surround it and encourage more jobs to be advertised as suitable for flexible working (Taylor, 2017). These recommendations were largely accepted, but progress has been slow here too.

Flexible working as a concept is about many things. At its most basic definition, it is about individual employees making applications for changes to their working hours – usually to step outside of the default working model in some way. It is about supporting working parents, utilizing different working patterns and looking at new ways of working. But it is also much, much more than that. Flexible working is about rethinking how we work at a fundamental level. It is about empowering employees to define how, where and when they work best, trusting them, and providing them with the autonomy to create that for themselves. It is about abandoning old-fashioned command and control-style management, and replacing it with collaboration and communication. It is also about recognizing that everyone is an individual with their own unique values, wants, needs and personal obligations, and that pursuing these alongside their work does not make for less productive and committed employees. It is about shifting the employment relationship from parent–child to one that is truly adult–adult. Flexible working is about seeing the whole person. It is about recognizing that what really matters is that the necessary work is done and done well, and if that takes place around an individual's caring needs, other responsibilities or even a yoga class, that is just fine. Flexible working is about truly inclusive working environments.

Flexibility is at the very heart of the future of work. All organizations urgently need to rethink their traditional approaches to work and working hours and embrace the many benefits of greater flexibility. To fail to do so is not only a missed opportunity, but a potentially significant business risk.

There is perhaps one more reason to introduce flexible forms of working, and this is one that relates less to business outcomes, costs and benefits, but to something that is to some extent less tangible and measurable. Simply, introducing flexible working is the right thing to do. Many of our workplaces lack diversity, equality and inclusivity. Too many potential workers are locked out of the default working model entirely, or unable to fulfil their potential in workplaces that hold fast to traditional ways of work and old-fashioned attitudes. Some work and workplaces are inherently unhealthy, whether that is a result of poor organizational culture, over-work or poor job design. This idea of flexible working as the right thing to do could perhaps be called the *social justice* case. We have become used to this terminology in recent years in relation to discussions about corporate social responsibility and inclusion. A revolution in flexible working could lead to real change for individuals and for society, by tackling stereotypes, opening up opportunities, improving workplace wellbeing and delivering autonomy and empowerment. Whilst such an argument may hold less influence in the boardroom, these are nevertheless important considerations in the case for flexible working.

I have outlined many reasons why it is time for organizations to take flexibility seriously, but there is perhaps one primary driver that supersedes the rest: increasingly, this is how people want to work. Flexibility is an employee-driven movement. Employees want a new deal. The psychological contract is changing.

This is not to say that flexible working is not without its challenges, many of which we will discuss later in this book. In organizations today, there are very few easy answers to complex problems. Flexible working has many benefits, but it can also have negative impacts when not managed or implemented properly. It can be a potential key to unlocking greater gender equality, but may perpetuate problematic gender norms too. It can benefit employee wellbeing in some circumstances, but in others have unintended – and potentially negative – consequences too. Some of these challenges arise directly from issues of poor progress, patchy implementation and mixing old and new working models. With a true flexible working revolution, these challenges can be overcome.

Flexible working is still 'other', different and non-standard. This book will make the argument that now is the time for change. It is time for what Fagan *et al* (2006) describe as 'a vision of a workplace of the future... where workers can have not only a work–life balance but also some control over their working lives and where employers can gain a competitive edge.' Inherent in this explanation is the idea that with flexibility everyone benefits.

We have the technology. Employees undoubtedly have the desire. All parties to the working relationship can benefit from its adoption. The time for a flexible working revolution is now.

Aims of the book

This book has two broad aims. Firstly, it will seek to make the case that all organizations should take flexible working seriously, and that the time to do so is right now. It aims to provide evidence to support this view from a range of sources, from academic research to real-life case studies detailing the practical work of very different types of organization. The book will also explore the challenges and issues presented by flexible working, and how these might be overcome.

The demand for flexible working is a trend of its own but to understand it fully, we must also view it within the context of broader, global changes relating to the world, and future, of work. Work has changed significantly in recent decades, change that has been partly fuelled by the increasing capability and availability of technology. But in many respects *how* we work has not changed perhaps as much as it could have and we have held fast onto the old ways of working. We continue to undertake the rush-hour commute, to have face-to-face meetings and hold learning in a classroom, when other (potentially better or more effective) ways of working are available to many of us. Arguably, the very real resistance towards flexible working is just one more example of this broader failure to adapt – albeit this is not true of all businesses. The first part of the book will explore these issues in depth, considering the many lenses through which flexible working can be viewed, as well as the various business-related benefits.

The second aim of the book is to provide a highly practical approach to the design, implementation, communication and evaluation of flexible working strategies that can be used by all types of organization. This book will enable organizations, managers, leaders and human resources functions to get ready for a more flexible future through the provision of the evidence base for flexibility, as well as thorough case studies, guidance and template tools and documents. This book has been written to meet the needs of both the HR practitioner and the business leader who wish to introduce flexible working in their own organization.

Structure of the book

The book is split into two parts. Part One focuses on the reasons and business case for flexible working, considering a variety of perspectives, research and potential benefits. It will consider flexible working in the context of not only family-friendly support for employees, but also sustainability, employee wellbeing, employee engagement, inclusion and the attraction and retention of talent. It will also describe the many forms of flexible working, the statutory framework in which it operates (including its limitations), as well as its broader positioning within the changing future of work. Finally, it will also consider the barriers to and myths associated with flexible working – and how they can be overcome. Part One also includes case studies from organizations of varying sizes and complexity who are already embracing flexible working opportunities.

Part Two of the book will focus on preparing organizations for a move towards a more flexible future and practical issues of implementation. It will set out how an organization can move from a place of compliance (with the legal framework) to one of culture; an organization in which flexible working is not simply tolerated but embraced, and its benefits fully realized. Part Two will also set out the building blocks of flexible cultures. As well as providing a range of tools and templates that the reader can adapt for their own particular circumstances, this part will also consider good practice in respect of policy development and drafting, communication and awareness raising for flexible working strategies, manager training and development, and a range of practical options for enabling and supporting flexible working and, in due course, measurement of success and progress. Each chapter includes a brief Next Steps section, clearly setting out the actions that can be taken to support implementation.

By the conclusion of the book, the reader who wishes to embrace flexible working will have everything that they need in order to do so.

References

CIPD (2019) *Flexible Working Practices*, www.cipd.co.uk/knowledge/ fundamentals/relations/flexible-working/factsheet (archived at https://perma.cc/ G5MS-LFGJ)

Clarke, S and Holdsworth, L (2017) *Flexibility in the Workplace: Implications of flexible working arrangements for individuals, teams and organizations*, Acas

Fagan, C, Hegewisch, A and Pillinger, J (2006) *Out of Time: Why Britain needs a new approach to working-time flexibility*, Trades Union Congress, www.researchgate.net/publication/286447808_Out_of_Time_-_why_Britain_ needs_a_new_approach_to_working-time_flexibility (archived at https://perma.cc/ B87P-XQRV)

Taylor, M (2017) *Good Work: The Taylor Review of Modern Working Practices*, assets.publishing.service.gov.uk/government/uploads/system/uploads/ attachment_data/file/627671/good-work-taylor-review-modern-working- practices-rg.pdf (archived at https://perma.cc/W4HQ-N7QQ)

Timewise (2019) *Should employers be required to consider flexible recruitment? Yes, but...* timewise.co.uk/article/should-employers-be-required-consider- flexible-recruitment/ (archived at https://perma.cc/TY78-HZAV)

XpertHR (2018) */Flexible Working Policies and Practice Survey 2018*, XpertHR

The case for flexibility

Part One of this book will begin by considering exactly what is meant by the term 'flexible working', the various forms of work flexibility in common use and the UK statutory framework in which it operates. It will then go on to consider the broader benefits of flexible working, issues of demand and availability, and then finally it will explore common barriers to flexible working and the myths associated with it and those who undertake it.

This section of the book will also review a range of evidence about flexible working, drawing particularly on academic research and industry survey data to provide readers with the information that enables them to make an evidence-based case for flexible working in their own organization.

01

Flexible working

An overview

What is flexible working?

Exactly what do we mean when we use the term 'flexible working'? It is undoubtedly a broad expression that means different things to different people. It often, somewhat unhelpfully, invokes ideas of part-time or re-duced-hours working, but there is much more to flexible working than simply a reduction in contractual hours. Flexible working does refer to part-time work, but it can also refer to a range of other changes to the traditional arrangement of work, as well as increased worker control over when and where their work takes place. Flexible working can also be seen as a shift; a shift from the employer being in complete control of working hours and patterns, to a state where the employee has achieved a degree of control for him- or herself.

In its broadest sense flexible working is any form of working pattern that sits outside the norm for the organization concerned. For many organiza-tions and their workers, that norm is Monday to Friday, 9 to 5 – or some-thing very similar. This is what this book refers to as the default model of work. There are many forms of flexible working, some of which are better understood and more commonly used than others. Some of these forms of flexibility have long been in use, whereas others have developed in recent years, becoming possible only through the advent of enhanced technology. How we define flexible working has evolved too; work can be flexible across several dimensions including when, where and how particular work is undertaken.

'When' (sometimes referred to as time flexibility) relates to the hours of work, both in terms of how many hours are worked in total as well as the timing of them. There are varying degrees of worker autonomy in relation to time flexibility, from complete employee control over when work is undertaken to systems with detailed constraint such as flexi-time combined with core hours. 'Where' work is undertaken (or location flexibility) has in particular been influenced by technology advances in recent years; many workers are now able to undertake their full range of duties anywhere with a wifi connection. Work can take place in the office, a home, a co-working space, a client's premises, a train or a coffee shop. Workers have the potential to be increasingly untethered from a physical space – where of course the organizational culture permits. Finally, there is 'how' work is undertaken. This can be categorized again into methods for undertaking as well as 'how much' work is undertaken.

On a practical level, flexible working arrangements can be both formal (agreed by way of the contract of employment, often via an organization's internal policy or statutory process) or informal (agreed locally between an employee and their immediate line manager, on a regular or ad hoc basis). The approach taken in each case is very much related to the culture of the organization, and the extent to which flexible approaches to work are enabled and encouraged.

There are many reasons why people work flexibly, and the drivers behind it can vary depending on the nature of the particular flexible working arrangement. The 2019 CIPD *Working Lives* survey looked into why people work flexibly. Surprisingly perhaps, and contrary to the stereotype of who personally wants to use flexible working, providing care for children or other relatives amounted to just under a quarter of reasons for those surveyed. Other reasons included more leisure time (more associated with compressed hours working) undertaking education or training, illness or disability, and the reduction in commuting time (with 12 per cent of workers stating this as their primary reason for working flexibly). The data regarding childcare is perhaps lower than might have been expected, at least according to the myths about flexible working, but this data was highly gendered. Of those who stated this as their main reason, only 13 per cent of the respondents were men as compared to a quarter of women.

Forms of flexible working

There are many different ways in which employees can undertake and organizations can offer flexible working. This section summarizes the typical forms of flexible working arrangements in common use.

Part-time/reduced-hours working

Part-time working is usually defined as any agreed contractual hours that are fewer than the typical working week for the relevant organization. According to the OECD data, in 2018 part-time employment amounted to just over 23 per cent of total employment in the UK (OECD, 2019). Hours may be worked over any pattern, including working fewer full days or undertaking shorter working days over a normal (usually five-day) working week. Part-time working remains the most common form of flexible working, particularly amongst female employees. This is generally considered to reflect our gendered society where women still undertake the majority of childcare and domestic labour.

Job-share

A typical job-share takes place when two individuals share a full-time role with equal responsibility for its duties. Some organizations have specific requirements or policies around job-share arrangements, such as the parties providing cover for each other during holiday periods. Others will allow the participating individuals to manage their own arrangements. The job-share may or may not be an equal split in terms of hours or days of work. Employees may split the responsibilities of the role completely (perhaps based on the specific skills or experience of the participants), or take joint responsibility for all of the work undertaken. Some job-share arrangements have a crossover or handover period where both parties have a defined time, such as a few hours or half a working day, when they are both in the workplace together; this can therefore slightly increase employer costs when compared to one full-time employee. Challenges of job-sharing can include effective communication between the parties and the need to ensure that the sharers are taking equal responsibilities and workloads.

Job-sharing as a form of flexible working can be underused. Managers can feel that a job-share arrangement means that they personally will have double the work with two employees to manage, review and develop. The success of a job-share relies to a large extent on the parties who are sharing the role. They will need clearly agreed ways of working as well as effective methods of communication. Practical issues can arise if one party leaves the organization in terms of securing a replacement. Conversely, when job-shares work well, the employer can benefit from two engaged and productive employees. Like part-time working, job-shares are often undertaken by female workers.

Compressed hours

Employees who work compressed hours typically work the normal full-time working week undertaken by their organization, but do so over a period other than five standard working days, for example, four or four-and-a-half days. This can have the benefit for employees of reduced commuting (for a four-day pattern) and potential reduced childcare costs. It does, however, lead to longer hours in the office on working days and means that employees are unavailable on one day a week, which may indicate why it is not currently a widely used form of flexible working.

Nine-day fortnight

Similar to compressed hours, full-time hours are worked over nine days rather than the more traditional 10, with employees working a longer working day on each of the nine days to allow for a non-working day. In practice, the non-working day is often a Friday, although it does not have to be. Some organizations adopt a nine-day fortnight as a standard operating model. The organization does not normally close on non-work days with the actual day off varying from employee to employee. This pattern has the benefit of reduced commuting but does not have the same long-day implication of compressed hours as the additional time is spread over nine and not four days. This form of flexible working can be undertaken on an individual as well as an organizational basis. From a talent attraction and retention perspective, this particular arrangement is extremely valuable – the opportunity to have a day off every two weeks without any impact on pay is an attractive employee benefit that may not be easily replicated at another organization.

Annualized hours

Annualized hours are similar to compressed hours. The employee is contracted to a set number of hours and paid in equal increments although the actual worked hours may vary week to week or month to month. This can be linked to seasonal demand. For example, an organization with high demand on the approach to Christmas may require employees to work more hours in November and December, but fewer during quieter summer months. Annualized hours sometimes include some 'core hours' that are required each week or day.

Part-time, term-time

Employees who have a part-time, term-time arrangement do not work during school holidays. Depending on the nature of the agreement between employee and employer, this may just be the long summer holiday or all of the school holidays throughout the year. Salary is reduced accordingly but is still paid in equal instalments throughout the year. This arrangement can work well for organizations that have quieter periods during the summer months and is popular in educational institutions. Employees can benefit significantly from the reduction in childcare costs.

Flexi-time

Flexi-time typically refers to arrangements whereby an employee can be full- or part-time, and is required to work during daily core hours (often 10am–4pm) but their actual start and finish times are at the discretion of the employee, and may even vary day to day. Some organizations accompany flexi-time with 'time off in lieu' (TOIL) arrangements where employees can work more hours each day than their contractual obligation and then take that time in lieu through an agreed process. Most organizations develop their own policies and processes around the operation of flexi-time arrangements, some of which have a greater degree of employee autonomy than others.

Remote/homeworking

This simply means working from a location other than the normal workplace – usually the home. It is also sometimes referred to as 'teleworking'. Remote working allows for what Cooper and Hesketh (2019) call a 'distributed working day' – one where employees can work according to their personal orientation rather than 9 to 5 – assuming their organization permits it. Remote working can take place for the entire working week, where the employee rarely attends the workplace in person and is therefore managed remotely, or just for some of their working pattern. Patterns can be fixed (a set number of days per week or month) or variable/ad hoc. Again, many organizations have policies and processes around how homeworking operates in practice. This particular pattern is good for sustainability and well-being (reducing the carbon footprint of commuting as well as reducing commuting costs and stressors) and can help employees to have greater control and autonomy over their work. Homeworking can also provide a welcome respite from the busyness of the much-criticized open-plan office. It does, however, present a number of practical implications that organizations need to assess, including issues such as insurance, reimbursement of expenses, health and safety, and data protection. Homeworking is on the increase – a TUC survey in May 2019 found that over the last decade there has been an increase of over 27 per cent of the number of homeworkers, and a number of studies associate it with higher levels of job satisfaction (TUC, 2019a).

Staggered hours

In this case, employees work at different start, finish or break times to what is typical for the organization. For example, rather than working 9 to 5, an employee may work 7 to 3 to avoid peak commuting hours, or take a shorter lunch break to allow for an earlier finish. This can be operated on a fixed or rotating basis.

Self-rostering

This is typically used in environments where employees work shifts. Employees work either full- or part-time and are delegated responsibility within their team for determining what shifts each of the team work. Some organizations will simply refer to this as 'shift swapping'. Most organizations operating a self-rostering system will have a policy or process and agreed parameters that must be adhered to. This form of flexible working can provide control to employees who might otherwise have more limited flexible working opportunities than other workers – for example, a warehouse operative or security guard would be unable to work from home.

Zero-hours contracts

Zero-hours contracts are a form of flexibility, albeit a contentious one. Employees engaged on a zero-hours contract will have a formal contract of employment but no guarantee of a given (or indeed any) number of hours each week or month. In recent years zero-hours contracts have been criticized for providing precarious employment and exploiting workers. This particular form of flexibility is concerned with employees themselves being flexible, rather than flexibility provided for them by the organization – and it often seems that the employer benefits from this form of flexibility more than the employee. Research, however, suggests that some workers do value this form of flexibility (CIPD, 2013). In the case of zero-hours contracts, often the flexibility offered is more favourable to the organization than the employee, and the uncertainty they cause for workers may well negate the benefits more commonly associated with other forms of flexible working. Where an organization chooses to offer zero-hours contracts, it is good practice to guarantee a minimum number of hours that will be offered and state parameters around how arrangements will work in order to provide some certainty and security to employees.

Career breaks/sabbaticals

More common in some professions and industries than others, career breaks and sabbaticals are agreed periods of time away from work (ranging from a few months to a few years) during which the contract of employment typically continues but the employee does not receive any pay or benefits. At the end of the break the employee will return to their previous post. This time away from work can be undertaken for any reason and organizations will differ in their overall approach to the rules of career breaks. For example, some policies will preclude the individual from taking other paid employment during a career break. Some organizations also use career breaks as a reward for long service and include it as part of an employee benefits package. There can be many benefits to a career break. It can allow employees to take time out for a range of personal reasons such as undertaking a period of learning, providing care or travelling. The organization can retain an individual who might otherwise have left the business to pursue these non-work goals. In a world where employees will be working much later in life, career breaks may become more popular in the future.

Phased retirement

Typically, phased retirement involves the reduction of hours on a phased, reducing basis, as the individual approaches retirement. The length of the phasing will vary depending on the agreement reached between the individual and their organization and can include reducing hours over months or even years.

Alternative forms of flexible working

As we can see, flexible working comes in many forms. Many of the forms of flexibility detailed here so far are a form of permanent employment with a single employer – a working pattern negotiated or agreed that typically sits outside the Monday to Friday, 9 to 5 default. However, these are not the only trends currently being seen in the workforce in relation to flexibility. Forms of working that sit outside the default are sometimes seen in the nature of the employment relationship, the employee benefits provision and even ways of working. Some forms of flexibility or peripheral working are outside the scope of this book, but are nonetheless a form of workforce flexibility. Sometimes, workers choose (or may feel forced into) these non-standard forms of working because they are unable to access alternative working arrangements with their employers.

One such trend is the rise of self-employment. More people are undertaking self-employment (over 4.8 million workers in the UK in 2017 according to the Office for National Statistics) or a portfolio career (sometimes called a 'slashie' because of the slash dividing the different roles – for example, 'I am an Uber driver/barista') where people have more than one job that may be unrelated to each other and which may or may not be permanent forms of employment (Hot Spots Movement, 2019). 'Gig economy' (again often a form of self-employment) is another term that has come into increasing use and typically refers to workers taking multiple short-term assignments ('gigs'). One form of such gigs is sometimes known as 'platform working' where an online platform is used to connect workers to work. Examples include Uber driving or food delivery apps like Deliveroo. The aforementioned Taylor report has called for greater clarity in the law in relation to the rights of these atypical workers (Taylor, 2017).

Employee benefits

Flexibility can also sometimes be seen through the provision of employee benefits. In recent years it has become increasingly popular to allow employees the option to purchase (and sometimes sell) additional annual leave.

Some organizations also allow what are known as 'duvet days'. These are an allowance of days (usually just one or two per year), often added on to an annual leave allowance, where employees can simply opt to take the day off if they do not wish to attend work for any reason. There is no requirement to provide prior notice and employees can simply stay under their duvet – hence the name.

These are not typical forms of flexible working, and certainly fall outside the statutory framework, but they do represent other examples of employers empowering their employees to have more flexibility and choice about how often they work, as well as their work–family life balance.

Hot-desking

Another workplace trend popularized in recent years is 'hot-desking'. In this concept, employees do not have a permanent workspace allocated to them. Instead, the employer provides a range of (usually) open-plan spaces for people to use as they see fit – the idea being that employees can simply use whichever desk is free for the time that they need it. Hot-desking can also be combined with remote or homeworking. A primary motivation for the introduction of hot-desking is the ability for organizations to reduce office space and therefore reduce costs, although the approach is not always popular with employees.

Formal vs informal working patterns

In practice many organizations operate a whole range of working patterns for many reasons and working patterns can often evolve during employment. Some people want or need permanent flexibility; others need it just for a specific or short period of time. Much flexible working is informal, and this can bring both benefits and challenges. In a mature organization with high levels of trust and where relationships between managers and team members are strong, informal flexibility can work well. Employees can be enabled to work in the way that works best for them. Informal flexible working can, however, be problematic in two ways. Firstly, it is invisible to the organization and cannot be measured or monitored, which may lead to unfairness or inconsistency of approach. Secondly, employees with informal arrangements can be vulnerable in the event of a line manager change.

Formal flexible working requests will usually amount to a permanent change to terms and conditions of employment for the employee. This process can be time-consuming and lead to a rigidity of approach as well as having the unintended consequence of reducing ad hoc flexibility. However, it does provide employees with certainty and security.

There is no one 'best' type of flexible working arrangement and no one single way to approach its implementation. Not all forms of working will suit every organization and some are more suited to particular jobs types and professions than others. A successful flexible working arrangement is one that is mutually beneficial and fits the context of the organization and role – a subject to which we will return in later chapters.

Flexible working and the law

In the UK, employees have a statutory right under the Employment Rights Act 1996 (as amended by the Employment Act 2002) to make a request for flexible working, subject to meeting certain criteria. The legislation was first introduced in 2003 by the then Labour government. Initially, the right applied only to parents of children under six or disabled children up to the age of 18. At the time of its introduction, the primary aim of the legislation was the provision of support to working parents and encouraging women to return to the labour market after having children. The right to request flexible working was later amended in 2007 to include carers of 'near relatives', but after some debate, still not the parents of older children. In 2010 the Conservative Party pledged in its manifesto to extend the right to request flexible working to parents of children under the age of 18, which it subsequently introduced after coming to power. Finally, in 2014 the right was extended to all employees, regardless of status, by way of the Children and Families Act. At the same time, this legislation also replaced a formally complex and statutory procedure with a simpler requirement to consider requests 'reasonably'.

This early framing of flexible working as being a benefit for working parents (initially of young children) and those with caring responsibilities has had long-term repercussions for the acceptance of flexibility, as we shall explore later.

Should an individual wish to make a request for flexible working, the eligibility criteria must first be satisfied. The individual must be an employee of the organization in the legal sense of the word; the right to request flexible working and its associated processes do not apply to atypical workers such as contractors, agency staff or the self-employed. The employee must also have 26 weeks continuous service with their employer before a request can be made, and only one request can be made in a rolling 12-month period. The employer may, however, choose to apply their own policy that exceeds these minimum statutory requirements and many now choose to do so. In their application, the employee may make a request to change the hours that they are required to work, the times that they are required to work and/or where they work.

The legislation sets out a framework both for the making and considering of requests. Employees should put a request in writing to their employer, outlining the working pattern that they are seeking and the date from which they wish it to be effective. They should consider any potential impacts of their request on the organization and include details within their application as to how they believe these impacts can be overcome, as well as make a formal declaration that they have not already made a request in the previous 12 months.

The legislation then requires the organization (or typically, in practice, the employee's line manager) to consider the employee's request in a reasonable manner and within a reasonable time frame.

The employer, upon receipt of the application, can simply decide to agree to the request, in which case they should communicate this to the employee and detail the new terms and conditions of employment along with the effective commencement date. When a request is accepted, it amounts to a permanent change to the contract of employment between the parties and neither can unilaterally change those terms in the future without going through formal due process. The employee does not have the right to return to their previous working pattern (without a new formal agreement) and the employer cannot require them to do so. When the legislation provided for flexible working only for parents of children under the age of six, it was not unusual to find employers who believed that flexible working arrangements would terminate at a given point, but this is not the case, either previously or today.

If the request cannot be immediately agreed, a meeting must take place with the employee to discuss the request – in practice this will normally be undertaken by the employee's line manager. A decision must then be made to either accept or reject the request.

Where it is not clear initially whether a proposed working arrangement will be successful or suitable, an employer may offer the employee a trial period of the proposed new working arrangements. The length of a trial period is not specified in law and may be agreed by the parties, and can be for as long as is necessary to genuinely assess the impact of the proposed working pattern. During a trial period there is no change to the terms and conditions of employment and in the event a trial is not successful after its conclusion, the employee will revert to their former pattern of working. This will amount to a rejection of a request (see below) and therefore if the organization offers an appeal under their internal processes, this should also apply in these circumstances.

If, following due consideration (or an unsuccessful trial period), the employer decides to decline the request for flexible working, they may do so only for one or more reasons from a prescribed list. These are:

- the burden of additional costs;
- a detrimental effect on ability to meet customer demand;
- an inability to reorganize work amongst existing staff or recruit additional staff;
- a detrimental impact on quality or performance;
- insufficiency of work during the periods the employee proposes to work;
- planned structural changes;
- such other grounds as may be specified in regulations made by the Secretary of State.

The reason upon which the employer is relying in order to reject the request must be stated in writing to the employee.

Although the employer has discretion in the consideration of flexible working requests, it has been established via case law that a failure to reasonably agree to requests can amount to discrimination under the Equality Act 2010 and therefore an employee may bring a claim for discrimination against their employer. They can do so whilst continuing in employment, and there are no costs incurred by the employer from this. There is no limit on compensation awards for discrimination claims in the Employment Tribunal and compensation award may also be made for injury to feelings.

There is no statutory right of appeal against a rejection of a flexible working request, although this is included in many organizations' internal policies. The entire process must be concluded within three months, including the right of appeal where offered.

A supporting Acas Code of Practice (Acas, 2013) on flexible working provides additional guidance to employers. This Code sets a number of recommendations to employers, including:

- arranging to talk to an employee as soon as possible after receiving their written request (unless they are going to simply agree it, in which case a meeting is not necessarily required);
- discussing the employee's request with them in private;
- allowing the employee to be accompanied to any meetings by a work-based colleague or a trade union representative (this is also not a statutory right under the legislation but is typically included in many workplace policies);
- considering requests carefully, including giving thought to the potential benefits of the requested changes and weighing them carefully against any potential business impacts;
- informing the employee of the decision in writing as soon as possible – but certainly within the prescribed three-month time period;
- allowing the employee to appeal against the decision to another manager if the request is rejected.

In addition to the right to request flexible working, employees have a further legal right not to be subjected to any detriment because they have done so.

An employee has the right to bring a claim in the Employment Tribunal (in addition to the potential ground of complaint for discrimination, discussed above) against their employer on the grounds that the employer has failed to comply with its duties under the relevant legislation (such as to deal with the request within three months or in a reasonable manner), or that it has based its decision to reject the request on incorrect facts. In the event that the Tribunal finds that the complaint is well founded, they may make a declaration to that effect and either require the employer to consider the request again or pay compensation to the employee. The maximum compensation that can be awarded is eight weeks' pay, capped at the prevailing statutory maximum set annually by government. If an employee does bring Employment Tribunal proceedings against their employer in relation to a flexible working request, the Tribunal may take into account any failure of the employer to follow the recommendations of the Acas Code.

Further potential changes to flexible working legislation are under consideration. In 2019 the government began consulting on a range of potential changes relating to working family legislation, including flexible working. One of these potential changes is creating a duty for employers to consider whether a job could be undertaken on a flexible basis prior to advertising it, as well as the requirement for organizations to publish their flexible working policies. The consultation has concluded but the government is yet to publish its intentions.

This chapter sets out the minimum legal requirements to which an organization must adhere. In practice, many choose to go above and beyond the statutory minimum and improve their offering through their policy approach. Employment law can only have a limited impact by itself – employees also need to feel that they can make use of their rights and that there will be no career or other consequences from doing so. Without this, legal rights are meaningless.

The statutory framework set out here has a number of limitations contained within it that have resulted unintentionally in barriers to the effective implementation of flexible working. Later chapters will explore how organizations can improve upon the legal requirements and overcome its inherent challenges.

Whilst this chapter has focused on the legal requirements (within the UK specifically) for flexible working this is not the only way that employees can access flexible working arrangements. Many employees do not make formal requests through an internal policy; they simply agree informal arrangements with their line manager. This might be ad hoc (such as an occasional request to spend a day working from home) or something more structured. Informal arrangements may not require changes to contractual terms and conditions of employment, and therefore do not necessarily require the level of formality (or HR processes) of formal requests. As it is often unrecorded it is difficult to estimate how widespread this sort of flexibility is across the workforce, or even within a specific organization. Interestingly, one study has indicated that informal working arrangements lead to enhanced performance when compared to colleagues who have formalized and contractual flexible working arrangements via internal policies. Although the reasons for this are not entirely clear it is possible that the process itself influences this outcome (De Menezes and Kelliher, 2016). Arguably, informal flexible working reflects a more adult working relationship where employees and managers can work out for themselves effective ways of working that are mutually beneficial. This does, however, require a particular kind of organizational culture (and management competence) that may not exist in all workplaces.

As we can see, flexible working is indeed a wide and varied term. It encompasses many different forms of working, all of which have one thing in common: flexible working differs in some way from the default working model of (broadly) Monday to Friday, 9 to 5, so typical of many workplaces. As we will explore in later chapters, these differences bring with them both challenges and benefits, for individuals, managers and organizations alike.

Demand and availability

Recent years have seen a range of surveys and research undertaken into the demand for and availability of flexible working, by industry bodies, academics and campaign organizations. Broadly, this research indicates that the current demand for flexible working is outstripping the supply of available flexible jobs. This may indicate that the current legislation on flexible working isn't working or does not go far enough to deliver flexibility for those who want or need it.

Studies consistently find that flexibility is a benefit that employees and potential employees keenly value, potentially even more so than monetary rewards. For example, a poll by Investors in People asked employees to choose between a 3 per cent pay rise and other benefits; more than a third would prefer a more flexible approach to working hours (*HR Magazine*, 2013).

This isn't just a UK trend; 35 per cent of employees in the United States say that they would change their job to access more flexible working arrangements (Cooper and Hesketh, 2019) although adoption and usage of flexible working practices there is also described as slow and uneven (Munsch, 2016).

There currently appears to be a significant gap between those employees that want to work flexibly and those that can access the ability to do so – or certainly a gap between policy and practice. The Government Equalities Office suggests that many organizations are ostensibly committed to flexible working, but not providing it in practice (Nicks *et al*, 2019; Jones, 2019).

In January 2019 the CIPD published their Megatrends report, focusing on the UK and global picture of flexible working. Its findings suggest a mixed picture of flexible working availability, and an overall slow pace of change. The most popular form of flexible working in the UK is part-time work; now around a quarter of employees in the UK work less than full-time, with the majority (three-quarters) of them being women. Women are also more likely to work flexibly overall, often because they are combining work with care or domestic labour (CIPD, 2019a).

Homeworking is one form of flexible working that is on the increase (most likely as a result of improvements in technology enabling remote access to workplaces); globally it is estimated that more than two-thirds of people around the world work away from the office at least once every week, according to the International Workplace Group (IWG, 2019).

Other forms of flexible working such as compressed hours and nine-day fortnights are, however, much less utilized, with only around 2 per cent of UK employees using the latter working pattern (Wheatley, 2017). Public-sector workers are more likely to use flexible working arrangements than private-sector workers, and employees in larger organizations are more likely to have a wider range of flexible working arrangements available to them than those in smaller companies. Overall, the use of almost all forms of flexible working arrangements did not increase significantly between 2007 and 2013 (CIPD, 2019a).

Even when an organization does offer flexible working opportunities, not all employees can get the particular type of flexible working that they really want or need; 36 per cent of employees said that the particular type of flexible working that they wanted to work was not available to them in their current role (Working Families, 2018). Overall, it is estimated that around 87 per cent of employees would like to work flexibly at some level (Timewise, 2019). According to the CIPD, 32 per cent of employees would like to change their current working arrangements, the majority of whom would like to change their start or finish time, change the number of days they work each week or decrease the total number of hours they work (CIPD, 2019a). For example, the TUC estimate that around 4 million more workers would like to work from home even occasionally, but are not given the opportunity to do so.

The availability of flexible working is also influenced by seniority in organizations. CIPD research found that employees without management responsibility are most likely to work part-time, but are less likely to work other forms of flexible working than those who do undertake management roles. In comparison, senior and middle managers are mostly likely to report being able to work from home on a regular basis (31 per cent and 24 per cent respectively) when compared to more junior colleagues, and are also more likely to use flexible hours schedules. Junior managers are least likely to work flexibly at all (CIPD, 2016).

Where flexible working is available, there can be significant differences between exactly what can be accessed. Just under three-quarters of employees said that their workplace offered at least one form of flexible working arrangement. Some of these, however, are much more common in use than others – and who uses them is highly gendered, with men and women undertaking different forms of flexibility with different outcomes for them personally (Wheatley, 2017). So when we hear that flexible working is increasing, there is a complicated picture underneath the headlines and it does not necessarily follow that all organizations are offering it, or are offering the full range of the different forms of flexibility.

The majority of UK organizations now offer some forms of flexible working, with only around 10 per cent of employees saying that their employer offers no flexible working at all. Of those that have no access to flexible working, 78 per cent would like it. More than half the workforce would like to work flexibly in at least one form that is not currently available to them in their current place of work (CIPD, 2019c).

With regard to applications for flexible working, an online survey conducted by the TUC in August 2019 found that 1 in 3 applications for flexible working are turned down; the same survey showed that 3 in 10 employees say that their desire for increased flexibility would be one of the main factors in deciding whether to look for a new job opportunity (TUC, 2019b).

On the matter of flexible working for job seekers, every year flexible working consultancy Timewise produces the *Flexible Working Jobs Index*, a major study into job advertisements in the UK, reviewing 6 million jobs from over 300 online job boards. In 2019, this survey found that just over 15 per cent of jobs are advertised as potentially suitable for flexible working – a rise from the first Index in 2015 of 9.5 per cent. Almost half of those advertised flexible opportunities were for either part-time jobs or job-shares (which is another form of part-time working). Although the data indicate consistent growth in the expressed availability of flexibility, this amounts to just a few percentage points each year. The data also varies considerably when the salary is taken into account: flexible working is offered in 23 per cent of job adverts where the salary is less than £20,000 per annum but between £20–34,000 the availability of flexible jobs drops to 14 per cent. When it comes to higher-paid roles, the fastest growth rate for advertised flexible roles are those paying in excess of £60,000 per annum, trebling across the lifetime of the Index. The Index also highlights significant differences between sectors and role types (Timewise, 2019). From this we can conclude that not only offering flexible working but actively promoting it and encouraging it at the point of hiring can be a significant talent acquisition opportunity for all organizations.

These multiple sources of data indicate that there is a significant gap between the demand for flexible working and its availability to many workers. Where flexibility does exist, sometimes this amounts to just a few limited forms of flexibility such as part-time working, and not the wider range of potential forms of flexible working arrangements that could be employed.

We can therefore perhaps think of flexible working as something that exists on a spectrum. At one end of the spectrum, flexibility is actively discouraged, bringing with it negative consequences for those who work (or seek to work) flexibly. In the middle of the spectrum is tolerance; flexible working is permitted but not necessarily entirely accepted or normalized. It may exist under the radar or in the shadows. At the other end of the spectrum, flexibility is celebrated, actively encouraged and entirely open. The reader of this book may wish to reflect on where they think their own organization currently sits along this scale of flexibility.

KEY TAKEAWAYS

- There are many forms of flexible working, although the level of their use varies significantly. Flexible working can take place both through formal agreements or informal practices.

- Flexible working can take place through when people work (time flexibility), where they work (location flexibility) and in how work is done.

- Although flexible working is on the increase overall, this increase is slow and demand for flexible working is currently outstripping supply. This can present an opportunity for employers to embrace.

- The evidence about demand and availability supports the idea that it is time for a flexible working revolution.

- The statutory framework in the UK has evolved over several years, and is supported by an Acas Code of Practice which sets out how an organization can reasonably consider requests.

- The statutory framework is a minimum standard; organizations can and often do go above and beyond this standard in providing flexible working opportunities for their employees.

References

Acas (2013) Code of Practice: Handling in a reasonable manner requests to work flexibly, archive.acas.org.uk/media/3977/Code-of-Practice-on-handling-in-a-reasonable-manner-requests-to-work-flexibly/pdf/11287_CoP5_Flexible_Working_v1_0_Accessible.pdf (archived at https://perma.cc/E9VX-R967)

CIPD (2013) *Zero-hours Contracts: Myth and reality*, research report, CIPD, London

CIPD (2016) *Employee Outlook, Employee Views on Working Life, focus on commuting and flexible working*, CIPD, London

CIPD (2019a) *Megatrends: Flexible working*, CIPD, London

CIPD (2019b) *Working Lives Survey*, Wheatley, D and Gifford, J, CIPD, London

CIPD (2019c) *Cross Sector Insights on Enabling Flexible Working*, CIPD, London, www.cipd.co.uk/Images/flexible-working-guide-2019-v2_tcm18-58713.pdf (archived at https://perma.cc/676A-DYPS)

Cooper, C and Hesketh, I (2019) *Wellbeing at Work: How to design, implement and evaluate an effective strategy*, Kogan Page

De Menezes, LM and Kelliher, C (2016) Flexible working, individual performance and employee attitudes: Comparing formal and informal arrangements, *Human Resource Management*, Wiley

HR Magazine (2013) A third of employees would prefer flexible working over a pay rise, www.hrmagazine.co.uk/article-details/34-of-employees-would-prefer-a-more-flexible-approach-to-working-hours-than-a-pay-rise (archived at https://perma.cc/YEB8-GD5L)

Hot Spots Movement (2019) What are slashie careers?, www.hotspotsmovement.com/uploads/newsletters/slashie-careers.html (archived at https://perma.cc/93W4-WB83)

International Workplace Group (2019) Global Workplace Survey (2019) *Welcome to Generation Flex: The employee power shift*

Jones, L (2019) *Women's Progression in the Workplace*, Government Equalities Office

Munsch, C (2016) *Flexible Work, Flexible Penalties: The effect of gender, childcare and type of request on flexibility bias*, Oxford University Press

Nicks, L, Burd, H and Barnes, J (2019) *Flexible Working Qualitative Analysis: Organizations' experiences of flexible working arrangements*, Government Equalities Office

Office for National Statistics (2017) Trends in self-employment in the UK, www.ons.gov.uk/employmentandlabourmarket/peopleinwork/employmentandemployeetypes/articles/trendsinselfemploymentintheuk/2018-02-07 (archived at https://perma.cc/F9AH-S55U)

OECD (2019) *Part-Time Employment Rate (Indicator)*, doi:10.1787/f2ad596c-en, data.oecd.org/emp/part-time-employment-rate.htm (archived at https://perma.cc/CDP5-NEU8)

Taylor, M (2017) *Good Work: The Taylor Review of Modern Working Practices*

Timewise (2019) *Flexible Jobs Index 2019*, timewise.co.uk/wp-content/uploads/2019/09/TW_Flexible_Jobs_Index_2019.pdf (archived at https://perma.cc/4UX7-SZD3)

TUC (2019a) Homeworking up more than a quarter in last decade, TUC analysis shows, www.tuc.org.uk/news/homeworking-more-quarter-last-decade-tuc-analysis-shows (archived at https://perma.cc/EJ6X-27PD)

TUC (2019b) One in three flexible working requests turned down, www.tuc.org.uk/news/one-three-flexible-working-requests-turned-down-tuc-poll-reveals (archived at https://perma.cc/7RFH-7J4X)

Wheatley, D (2017) Employee satisfaction and use of flexible working arrangements, *Work, Employment and Society*, University of Birmingham

Working Families (2018) *The Modern Families Index 2018*, London

02

The benefits and challenges of flexible working

Flexible working has the potential to bring many benefits to organizations and individuals alike, and those benefits can apply to a whole range of employees, far beyond the working parents with whom it is too often predominantly associated. From the perspective of the individual employee it is easy to understand the appeal of more flexible forms of working. Flexibility can allow employees to have greater control over their working lives (reducing the risk of work-related stress and work–life conflict), enhance work–life balance, balance work with additional responsibilities such as care provision, and reduce the time and financial costs associated with commuting. These factors lie at the heart of increasing employee demand.

From an organizational perspective, flexible working can help with recruiting, engaging and retaining employees. It can lead to cost savings, support sustainability, improve diversity and inclusion, attract and retain talent, enhance productivity and improve employee wellbeing. These are subjects of interest to many employers.

This chapter will consider some of the main benefits of flexible working to each of the parties in the employment relationship, as well as highlighting some of the potential challenges for employees and organizations too. Later chapters will return to the subjects of inclusion and wellbeing and explore the benefits for each of these areas in more depth.

Many of the potential benefits discussed in this and later chapters are interlinked: organizations who undertake flexible working at scale often report more than one of them occurring together. One such organization is BT who has been leading in the flexible working space for many years, introducing their first initiatives in the 1980s. They estimate from their own internal research that productivity amongst their homeworkers is increased by between 15 and 31 per cent when compared to office-based colleagues. They also found that their homeworkers are less fatigued from commuting, and have reduced their overall overhead and property costs by an astonishing £500 million (Dwelly and Lake, 2008).

Headlines from flexible working research

Over the last few years, there has been a wide range of research undertaken into flexible working, including academic research, industry reports and surveys of flexible workers. Here are just a few of the headlines from that research, some of which will be explored in further detail later in this and the following chapters:

- CIPD research found that, according to employees, the top three benefits of flexible working most frequently cited are: it helps them to reduce the amount of stress and pressure they feel under (29 per cent); it enables better work–life balance (54 per cent); and it has been a factor in them staying with their current employer (28 per cent) (CIPD, 2016). Joint research by Working Families and Cranfield University found a positive relationship between flexible working and individual performance when considering both quality and quantity of work undertaken, and a positive influence on team-working (Working Families, 2009).

- Research suggests that employees who have access to flexible working arrangements report greater levels of job satisfaction than full-time employees, irrespective of whether the individual actually used the arrangements themselves (CIPD, 2019). A quarter of survey respondents said that being able to work flexibly enables them to be more productive at work and to pursue hobbies or other personal interests outside work (CIPD, 2016).

- The 9 to 5, Monday to Friday working pattern (what this book refers to as the 'default model') is not very popular amongst many workers. In fact, according to a YouGov poll, only 16 per cent of workers said this would be their preferred working pattern for a full-time job; 58 per cent would prefer to shift their working day earlier, favouring either a 7 to 3 or 8 to 4 pattern (*Personnel Today*, 2018).

- Flexible workers are much less likely to report being under excessive pressure at work than employees who don't work flexibly (29 and 42 per cent respectively, CIPD, 2016).

- Flexible working arrangements can reduce employee absence from work (Smeaton *et al*, 2014).

- A 2018 XpertHR survey asked employers what they believed were the main advantages to providing the opportunity of flexible working. Respondents cited a range of benefits, with the highest rated being improved employee retention and employee engagement. Other reported advantages included reduction in employee absence, increased productivity, a wider recruitment pool and better quality of applicants and promotion of equal opportunities (XpertHR, 2018).

- Employees who work flexibly say that they have better levels of work–life balance, and feel that they are more productive in terms of both the quality and quantity of their work (CIPD, 2016; 2019).

- Analysis by the RSA Action and Research Centre found a direct and statistically significant relationship between flexible working adoption and organizational performance, with key drivers being employee attitude and satisfaction (RSA, 2013).

- A survey of 111 employers by Industrial Relations Services (IRS) identified retention as the most widespread benefit of flexible working, with 74 per cent of respondents citing it as having improved in their organization as a result (IRS, 2009).

- 85 per cent of respondents to a 2019 survey of 15,000 business people globally said that their business is more productive as a result of flexible working (IWG, 2019).

These are all positive headlines. It should be noted, however, that flexible working can be a difficult subject to research, partly because of the breadth of the term and the many different forms that flexibility can take. The reasons why someone wants to undertake flexible working can also be relevant to its outcomes, as can the organization's own reasons for introducing flexible working arrangements. For example, working from home to reduce commuting (but maintaining full-time hours) can lead to different outcomes for employees, managers and organizations than those found when an employee reduces their hours as a result of childcare responsibilities. Different perspectives also emerge when we take issues like age and gender into account.

Talent

In the 1990s a well-known management consultancy coined the phrase 'the war for talent' to describe the idea that organizations would in the future need to compete aggressively to hire the talent that they need. This statement has long since become a cliché, but it is true to say that talent is a critical issue for every organization; all businesses need to recruit good people that have the necessary skills, experience, competencies and knowledge to do good work.

There are several aspects to talent. First of all is the ability to acquire the talent that an organization needs: individuals with the right skills and experience at the right times who can also demonstrate the right behaviour. This is the role of recruitment and selection, which includes the development of an attractive employer brand.

Once talented individuals are hired, they need to be motivated, developed, engaged, rewarded and effectively managed. These are tasks that fall to both the line manager and the wider organization through its people strategy and offerings. Finally, but also inextricably linked, is the need to retain talent. Flexible working can influence all areas of talent, and so we will now consider each in turn.

Recruitment

There is now a range of evidence from multiple studies that shows that the provision of flexibility is a key strategy for organizations who wish to attract talented individuals. Here are just a selection of the headlines from various studies and surveys:

- A 2010 survey found that 88 per cent of women and 81 per cent of men in the UK said that the ability to combine work and family is a very important factor when choosing their next job (Chung, 2018).

- Global research in 2019 by the International Workplace Group found that four out of every five respondents said that, given two similar job offers, they would turn down the one that did not offer flexible working (IWG, 2019).

- A further global Randstad survey of nearly 200,000 employees found that flexible working was one of the five most significant factors when looking for a new job (Randstad, 2016).

- Overall, 87 per cent of people say that they would like to work flexibly – but only 15 per cent of jobs are advertised as being open to flexible working arrangements (Timewise, 2019).

As we have seen from the discussion in Chapter 1 about demand and availability, demand for flexible working is high but availability is not. Offering flexible working can therefore open up entirely new talent pools from which organizations can recruit. Right now, despite the potential of flexible working, offering it remains a differentiating factor in the labour market – providing organizations with all the more reason to do so. From a business perspective, flexibility has another and perhaps overlooked benefit: offering flexible working can cost very little (if anything) in financial terms, especially when compared to other initiatives that organizations sometimes undertake in order to engage their workforce.

The organization Working Families is a UK-based work–life balance charity which encourages the use of its strapline 'happy to talk flexible working' on recruitment advertising on a job-by-job basis. Recruiting organizations can choose whether to make a simple statement to this effect, or go into detail about the specific forms of flexibility they may consider for each role. Whichever option is chosen, advertising flexibility can help to encourage candidates to apply for roles they might otherwise not have considered. Including a reference to flexible working on careers web pages or job advertisements can give candidates the permission to begin a conversation with the recruiting manager.

Of course, the rhetoric must also match the reality. It is not unusual for employees to report that information available during recruitment or induction indicated that the workplace was flexible and supported a range of working patterns – but that these promises were unfulfilled in practice when the individual started work.

It is not just external talent who need information on, or opportunities for, flexibility; when hiring, there are internal candidates to consider too. Employees with existing flexible working arrangements frequently report that opportunities for internal movement or progression can be limited as agreed flexible working arrangements are often not considered to be portable when applying for internal roles, unless the organization chooses to make this part of their flexible working policy. Internal candidates are a rich source of experience and organizational knowledge, but if organizations keep advertising their new opportunities as full-time and inflexible, existing flexible workers will remain an untapped talent pool.

As we have already seen with external recruitment, the majority of roles in the UK are advertised as full-time, 'standard' hours, and flexible options are rarely included (only 15 per cent of jobs were advertised as potentially suitable for flexible working in 2018). This can lead to qualified employees becoming 'stuck' in roles, sometimes working at levels lower than their skill set, experience or knowledge might otherwise demand. This is a particular issue for women who, as a result of a complex range of factors, are often the parent who reduces working hours following the birth of children.

Organizations can tackle this barrier with a range of simple measures. As well as adopting 'happy to talk flexible working' or equivalent straplines, they can expressly state that when applying for internal vacancies employees may apply on any existing flexible working pattern and this will be given due consideration, including a trial period, if they are the most suitable candidate. Any such approach will need to be accompanied by information and guidance for managers; they will need to understand the benefits to them of advertising roles as suitable for flexible working, and have their particular concerns about doing so addressed.

Retention

In addition to the potential opportunity of flexible working when it comes to talent acquisition, a failure to provide flexible working opportunities is also a talent retention risk. The demand for flexible working, combined with the issues of availability discussed in Chapter 1 suggests that providing flexible working will support the retention of employees and your ability to keep knowledge and skills within your organization. We know that the demand for flexibility is not related to one type of worker – it is desired across gender, age and job type. So, equally, retention is not about just retaining working women or mothers returning from maternity leave.

A 2019 survey undertaken by consulting firm Deloitte highlights this issue. They looked specifically at the experience of working 'millennial' fathers. Out of the survey respondents, one-third had changed jobs to achieve more flexibility, and a further third were considering doing so. Flexible working can be a powerful talent attraction tool when included in the employer brand mix. It is increasingly clear that employees who cannot achieve the desired level of flexibility or life–work balance at the existing place of work will seek opportunities elsewhere.

Although retaining staff is not just about parents, flexible working can undoubtedly help to retain women who are returning to work after maternity leave. One survey of 2,000 women found that nearly 1 in 5 (18 per cent) UK working mothers have been forced to leave their jobs because a flexible working request has been turned down – and many of them said that they felt their requests had not been given any genuine consideration (Workplace Insight, 2019). One organization that has used flexible working to support women returners is BT. They have a maternity return rate of 97 per cent, which they attribute to the availability of homeworking (Dwelly and Lake, 2008).

Retaining staff ensures that an organization also retains their knowledge and skills – and avoids the potentially high costs associated with recruiting and staff turnover. Simply put, if you don't offer flexible working to your employees, they may go and find an employer that does. Perhaps equally as importantly, as the next paragraph will demonstrate, those staff that are retained will also be more engaged and satisfied during the employment.

Employee engagement

Employee engagement is a term that was first used in the 1990s and is now very familiar to human resources professionals and business leaders alike. The idea of employee engagement quickly caught on and (despite being the subject of some academic criticism) became a standard part of people and HR strategies in organizations everywhere. In many respects, employee engagement builds on much earlier ideas about employee motivation and job satisfaction, both of which are also topics on which there are no shortage of theories, many of which span several decades.

Employee engagement is essentially about the relationship between the employee and the employer – something occasionally referred to as the 'psychological contract'. There is no single agreed definition of employee engagement, but an engaged employee is generally considered to be one who has a positive attitude towards their organization and is enthusiastic about their work. Although the idea of engagement as a concept is criticized, it remains undoubtedly popular with organizations. The underlying assumption upon which employee engagement is built is that an engaged (or satisfied) employee is more likely to be productive and an advocate for their organization. It is also often assumed (although evidence to support this point of view is subject to debate) that organizations with higher levels of employee engagement will financially and operationally outperform those who do not. Dr Amy Armstrong from Ashridge suggests this definition of an engaging workplace: 'An organizational climate where people choose to give the very best of themselves at work' (Armstrong *et al*, 2018).

In recent years it has become common practice for organizations to survey their staff on a regular basis with a view to finding out how engaged they are. There are many complex factors that influence engagement – it is after all a subjective issue. One key area in which there appears to be broad agreement is the role of line managers and leaders, and their significant influence on the employee engagement of the people that work for them. In 2009 the MacLeod report into employee engagement identified the manager as one of four critical enablers for employee engagement, describing an effective manager as someone who facilitates and empowers the people they manage as opposed to controlling or restricting them, who treats their staff with appreciation and respect, and shows commitment to developing and rewarding them (MacLeod and Clarke, 2009). It is not difficult to see where flexibility fits into this narrative. Flexibility is ultimately about empowerment, and the very opposite of control. Indeed, flexible working requires trust and for employees to be treated as individuals with their own needs, desires and obligations.

Where employee engagement theory tends to look at the employee/employer relationship, motivation theories consider intrinsic and extrinsic factors that drive employees to do their best. Theories about motivation have been plentiful for decades, some of them dating back to the early 1900s. Ultimately, motivation theories aim to explain people's reasons for doing something, both in general and in the workplace specifically. There is no single unifying theory of motivation, and ideas about what causes it have evolved over time. Early theories such as scientific management often focused on the idea that money was a key motivator, although we now understand individual motivation to be significantly more complex. A journey through the many theories of work motivation includes ideas ranging from social and physiological needs through to the role of achievement, recognition and growth, and even power and status. Some of the theories of motivation focus on the needs and expectations of individuals, others on what motivates people or what the outcomes of motivation are. Research has also paid attention to what can demotivate employees or dissatisfy them. Lack of perceived fairness, threats of punishment, job insecurity, poor work relationships or inadequate pay levels are just some of the factors that can reduce motivation and satisfaction.

Despite the many different ideas about motivation, there are some areas of agreement. Many people are motivated not by money or other similar extrinsic factors, but by factors such as responsibility, achievement, interesting and meaningful work, challenge and the opportunity for personal growth. A more recent and influential book on the subject by Daniel Pink, *Drive*, identified three factors that drive motivation in the workplace, with particular reference to the motivation of knowledge workers. Pink tells us that it is not financial rewards, as is often believed or espoused by some of the earlier motivation theories, but instead the opportunity for individuals to develop autonomy, mastery and purpose (Pink, 2018). Autonomy is of course about choice – the ability to have control over when, where and how we work best. This can be contrasted with a lack of control as an identified cause of work-related stress – a subject we will return to in Chapter 5 on wellbeing.

Here we can see how flexible working arrangements can contribute positively not only to the practical aspects of the life of employees but to their wider professional self, and as a result, organizational outcomes. As we discussed in the Introduction, flexible working at its broadest definition provides people with choices and options about their work and how they undertake it. Autonomy is at its heart. Other academics agree: 2017 research from the University of Manchester found that flexible working acts as a motivating factor, with employees who undertake flexible working patterns being more willing to give back to their organization (Clarke and Holdsworth, 2017). There is no one way to motivate an entire workforce; every individual responds to different incentives.. What motivates one person will not necessarily motivate (or even satisfy) someone else. It does appear, however, that offering flexible working can be one contributory factor. It aligns closely to ideas about job enrichment, variety, autonomy and responsibility and can help employees to shape their working life to fit their individual circumstances.

Motivation theories also have some similarities with ideas about what enhances employee satisfaction with their work. Job satisfaction is typically (and simply) defined as the extent to which an individual employee is satisfied with their work. Surveys have found that flexible workers are more likely than non-flexible workers to describe themselves as 'very satisfied' with their job. Interestingly, this enhanced job satisfaction also extends to employees who are *not* using flexible working arrangements but who do work for an organization where they are known to be available. Therefore, even the perception that the organization is supportive of flexibility can have a positive effect on both job satisfaction and organizational commitment (De Menezes and Kelliher, 2011).

Whether we use motivation, engagement or satisfaction as the main measure, flexible working does appear to generate positive benefits. As we can see from the headlines on flexible working research, there is now a body of evidence building that suggests the provision of flexible working will lead to increased levels of employee engagement and job satisfaction which will in turn be good for business. However, as with many other areas of flexible working research, the extent to which flexible working arrangements lead to greater overall satisfaction does seem to be influenced by the specific type of flexibility undertaken, with some forms of flexible working leading to better outcomes than others. Other factors are also relevant to satisfaction: some forms of flexible working have significant, positive effects on overall life satisfaction, but these patterns are highly influenced by gender. According to Wheatley (2017), flexi-time arrangements are associated with lower levels of life satisfaction amongst women but higher satisfaction amongst men. Women are more likely to undertake flexi-time with caring or other responsibilities, such as combining it with the school run. In contrast men do not necessarily combine flexi-time with other activities, which may be the differentiating factor in these varying impacts on satisfaction.

One organization that has invested significantly in flexible working in recent years is the National Health Service (NHS). For the NHS, flexibility is seen as a business critical issue, and their own internal research found that 92 per cent of staff said flexible working was important to them (NHS Inspiring Leaders Network, 2019). A 2011 study reviewed the impact of flexible working on levels of employee happiness within parts of the organization. Although a small sample size, the research found that flexible working was seen by employees to lead to them feeling pleased and cheerful, content and calm, with some survey respondents clearly making the link for themselves between flexible working and being happy. Overall happiness gave rise to additional discretionary behaviour and desirable performance outcomes (Atkinson and Hall, 2011).

However engagement is defined or measured, there is a general consensus that most organizations have an engagement problem. Although sectors, professions and countries will have their own patterns of engagement (as well as their own challenges) many employees are simply not engaged, a fact that has been found in many pieces of research. Gallup, one of the world's leading providers of employee engagement surveys, estimates that only 15 per cent of employees globally are highly engaged and enthusiastic about their work or workplace, a fact that they partly attribute to organizational resistance to change and failure to adapt to the changes made available by new technology, as well as the inability to meet the expectations of younger workers (Gallup, 2017). This provides further evidence for the argument that there is an urgent need for all organizations to focus on employee engagement in general – including a need to adapt traditional working practices, find new ways of working and meet the changing needs and wants of employees. Through these actions we can begin to close the engagement gap.

In summary, there are strong arguments to support flexible working as an important part of an organization's approach to talent management, including the attraction, engagement, motivation and retention of talented individuals. It can support job enrichment and levels of individual satisfaction. As we shall see next, it can also support those talented employees to be productive and perform well.

Performance

The business case for flexible working in respect of performance and productivity is now building, in contrast to the concern that can sometimes arise that it will actually have a negative impact in these areas. Here is just a sample of recent research into the subject:

- Research from the RSA suggests that flexible working can be a powerful driver of organizational performance, identifying benefits including innovation, skills utilization, motivation and productivity. Looking at innovation in particular, it appears that confidence in the innovative value of flexibility increases the more it is experienced. When interviewed on the subject, some employees highlighted how they feel that outside of the traditional workplace and its distractions it is easier for them to concentrate, think and be more creative. Many workers also reported that they are simply able to get more done in less time as a result of flexible working arrangements (RSA, 2013).

- Global research by the International Workplace Group found that 85 per cent of business people surveyed across 80 nations said that flexible working had made their business more productive (IWG, 2019). This is indeed a persuasive statistic, and there is plenty of other evidence from outside the UK that demonstrates these benefits are not limited to some countries or economies.

- An evidence review published by the Government Equalities Office in 2019 highlighted multiple studies from across the EU, Canada and the United States that consistently showed positive outcomes relating to performance, absenteeism, productivity, turnover and cost savings (Lyonette and Baldauf, 2019).

- A detailed two-year study by Working Families into several large organizations looked at the impact of flexible working on performance. This research took into account a range of measures including the views of flexible workers themselves and their managers and colleagues, and found that overall there was a positive relationship between flexible working and individual performance, particularly when comparing flexible workers with those undertaking more traditional patterns of work. The study also looked at performance from a variety of perspectives; the direct impact upon quantity of work undertaken by flexible workers, the quality of that work and the impact upon team-working. It then went on to consider additional indirect impacts on performance including job satisfaction, commitment and careers. The results were positive across all but one area of the study. Taking quality of work specifically, the vast majority of the respondents found that there was either no impact at all on productivity of performance, or an improvement. Only a very small minority (less than 5 per cent in all categories considered) believed there to be a negative impact. The study also found high levels of organizational commitment, increased job satisfaction and a positive impact on work–life balance, all factors that can indirectly influence individual performance. There was only one area of negative impact identified by the study, and that was a belief by managers and employees that working flexibly was harmful for careers, a subject to which we will return later and which does appear, sadly, to be based in reality (Working Families, 2009).

- The 2018 Working Families report into top flexible employers found that flexible and part-time employees outperformed their full-time colleagues; the percentage of top performance ratings for part-time and reduced-hours workers is higher than the percentage of top performance ratings across all staff, at 34 per cent compared to 14 per cent. Of course, not all organizations apply formal ratings to performance, but given the often quoted concern about whether flexible workers are as productive as their colleagues undertaking more traditional patterns of work, this is a persuasive statistic that suggests that this fear is unfounded.

The accumulating body of evidence in relation to performance and productivity, some of which is discussed here, can reassure senior leaders who are concerned about the potential impacts of flexible working on their organization's overall performance. It is, in fact, likely that supporting flexible working will have an overall positive impact, which, when combined with other benefits discussed in this chapter, is a compelling addition to the business case.

Cost savings

There are a number of ways that flexible working can help organizations to cut costs, including savings made through reducing sickness absence or absenteeism due to work-related stress and home responsibilities, staff recruitment and the costs associated with replacing leavers and training new staff.

Flexible working can also help to reduce costs in relation to office space. Enabling a range of working patterns, including remote working in particular, can reduce the amount of desk space required and create new ways of working within organizations. In the 2019 International Workplace Group survey 65 per cent of businesses said flexible working helps them to reduce either capital or operational expenditure (IWG, 2019).

As well as the potential cost savings that can be generated from adopting some form of flexibility, there are other financial considerations to take into account. Many of the initiatives or activities that employers undertake in order to attract, retain, engage, motivate and reward their people cost money. Consider the provision of employee benefits packages, the delivery of learning and development, reward and recognition schemes, wellbeing programmes and communication activities – each of which comes with potentially considerable costs. Often, flexible working costs nothing at all, or very little. This factor is often overlooked: it can be a critical way of engaging employees that requires little financial investment. Some flexible working arrangements such as compressed or annualized hours, flexi-time or working from home may have no cost to the organization and some patterns may even save money. When we consider the extent to which flexible working arrangements are valued by those that undertake them, flexible working might just amount to one of the most cost-effective talent solutions available. A 2019 global survey illustrated this point when it asked employees which workplace perks were the most important to them. Some 41 per cent replied 'flexible working', compared to a mere 6 per cent who appreciated an on-site gym, 6 per cent who valued free food at work and 2 per cent who favoured tuition fee reimbursement (WorkHuman, 2019). All of these employer-provided benefits are likely to cost significantly more than the provision of (sometimes small) amounts of flexibility.

Sustainability

Most organizations today are concerned with issues of corporate social responsibility and sustainability to some extent, whether this is for reasons of ethics or simply their brand and image. For some organizations it is a central part of their overall corporate strategy and approach to doing business. There is now increasing attention being paid to the potential of flexible working in supporting sustainability, particularly in relation to the impact on the environment of commuting, as well as reducing the need for real estate. Generally, the most relevant form of flexible working in terms of the environment is homeworking.

One emerging idea that could have a significant impact on the environment through reducing the carbon footprint of commuting is the four-day working week. This is less a form of flexible working as it is an idea about the fundamental future of work. In much the same way that in the early 20th century campaigners argued strongly for a reduced working week from six days to five, similar arguments are now being made that all employees should shift from five days per week to four. Whilst this might win favour with employees, whether the idea continues to gain traction or the support of business in particular will remain to be seen. Initial studies have demonstrated that there is real potential here for positive environmental impacts. In one survey, more than half of respondents said that they would drive their car less, most commonly reducing weekly mileage by between 10 and 19 miles. If the results were scaled up to apply to the whole of the UK, a national four-day working week could reduce the number of miles driven by employees travelling to work by 558 million each week and a reduction of car mileage by up to 9 per cent – leading to a significant reduction in fuel consumption (Nanda, 2019). Of course, a reduction in the overall working week may lead to other benefits such as improvements for individuals in respect of wellbeing and work–life balance as well as reduced childcare and commuting costs.

Outside of this possible future of a shorter working week, there are other ways that flexible working can support sustainability and help the environment. Homeworking may help to drive lower carbon emissions, not only through the reduction in commuting (mainly via cars) but also through the reduced need to heat and light office spaces. However, there is the potential that this will just shift the latter to the home instead. A further issue in calculating potential savings is what has been termed the 'rebound effect'. Carbon that may be reduced through fewer work journeys may result in the cars then being available for other use and journeys, or employees may choose to live in a different (potentially more remote) location if they don't have to live as close to their usual workplace – resulting in additional journeys or travel unrelated to work commuting (Dwelly and Lake, 2008). People may also use the time saved by reducing their commute to make other car journeys unrelated to commuting.

Some organizations have done their own analysis into the issue. As we noted earlier in this chapter, BT have experienced many benefits from introducing flexible working, and homeworking in particular. These benefits also extend to the environment. They estimate that as a result of reduced commuting, they have saved an equivalent of 12 million litres of fuel and a reduction in CO_2 emissions of around 97,000 tonnes (Dwelly and Lake, 2008).

Not everyone agrees that flexible working (and homeworking in particular) will make a real difference in this area. Stephen Glaister, Director of the Royal Automobile Club (RAC) Foundation, writing for the Smith Institute, argues that the relationship between homeworking and travel is complex. Even when benefits are realized, the RAC is forecasting the continued rise of car ownership and road travel, which would offset these benefits (Dwelly and Lake, 2008). This perhaps gives further support to the argument that we need a genuine flexible working revolution – a small number of employees working occasional days from home will not deliver the necessary environmental change, but significant numbers of employees working from home on a regular basis may.

The issue of sustainability is closely linked to technology. If the main benefit for the environment comes from reducing commuting (and therefore increasing levels of home and remote working), without the appropriate technology to enable that remote working the benefits cannot be fully realized. Effective homeworking needs to be combined with relevant technology including video- and phone-conferencing, online sharing and collaboration tools. Only by reducing the reliance on face-to-face meetings and communication can the potential environmental benefits of homeworking be attained.

Sustainability benefits are likely to be a long-term game. Currently those buildings that employees are commuting to still exist and will continue to need heating and lighting and other utilities all of which have a carbon footprint of their own, even if fewer people are occupying them as a result of homeworking. Only in time (and with significant changes to ways of working) can flexible working arrangements influence the size or construction of new buildings at all. To make a real difference to the environment there would need to be a complete shift in the economy towards homeworking.

This chapter demonstrates that many benefits of flexible working for all parties in the employment relationship are clearly established – and the evidence base continues to build. As the demand for and interest in flexible working continues to increase, this is an area that will attract further research in the future.

If there are so many evidenced benefits, why is there still so much resistance to adopting these new ways of working in some organizations and from some managers? Flexible working unfortunately remains beset by negative attitudes, resistant managers and outdated organizational models, some of which we will explore later in this chapter. There are also a range of myths associated with working flexibly, some of which we will explore in Chapter 6. Despite these problems, there are many organizations that are experiencing tangible benefits as a result of a flexible approach to working arrangements, as the following case study demonstrates.

CASE STUDY
Atkins Group

For the Atkins Group, there is no one single reason why they are passionate about flexible working; they recognize that it can bring them multiple business benefits from reducing real estate costs, attracting and retaining talent to improving employee engagement. Their flexible working agenda is also a central part of their inclusion strategy. In addition to these tangible benefits, Atkins also sees enabling flexibility as simply the right thing to do for their people. Feedback from employees suggests that they have got this right; through employee engagement surveys, employees have consistently rated the ability to work flexibly as one of the top three reasons they like working for the organization.

Atkins are not prescriptive in the forms of flexibility that they support. They offer almost every form available including part-time working, term-time working, job-shares, compressed hours, nine-day fortnights and variable start and finish times. They aim to be open-minded to any form of request made, even when there is no current organization precedent; their philosophy is to find a way to say yes to requests wherever possible.

The company has realized many benefits from their flexible working journey. Encouraging remote working has enabled them to reduce the size of their buildings estate, whilst still providing an effective hub for collaboration. Flexible working has also led to improved retention, particularly amongst women returning from maternity leave. Attrition of female returners has decreased from 19 per cent in 2013 to a low of 8 per cent and they have also seen a year on year increase of part-time working – including male part-time workers – by almost 10 per cent.

In order to enable and encourage flexible working, Atkins take a number of steps. They advertise all roles as open to flexible working and are happy to have conversations at the recruitment stage about the potential for flexible approaches. They have signed the Working Forward pledge to affirm their commitment to flexible working and working families. (Working Forward is a nationwide network, backed by some of the UK's leading businesses, to make workplaces as inclusive as possible.) Even when legislation only made statutory flexible working requests available to carers and parents, Atkins have always made it available to their entire workforce.

They work proactively to ensure that all employees are aware of the opportunities available to them, as well as with managers to help them understand the breadth of business benefits that flexible working can deliver. They run regular managers' talks which, as well as promoting those benefits, aim to address any concerns managers may have about the implications of flexible working and help them to develop the skills to manage flexible workers. Flexible working is championed by the internal parents' network, just one of a number of diversity networks operating across the organization. Atkins recognizes that this is not just an issue for parents; flexible working can benefit everyone. Senior leadership role modelling also plays a key part in acceptance and the company has seen a positive response to leaders being open about their own flexibility and balancing work and family life.

At Atkins, technology is a key enabler to working flexibly. Through the IT tools provided, employees are as effective in any location as they are in an office, meaning employees can work remotely – all helping towards reducing travel and improving sustainability.

Atkins aims to empower all their people to work flexibly and to be a truly best-in-class flexible employer.

Whether an organization can maximize the benefits of flexible working over any potential challenges and costs will to a large extent depend on their attitude towards it. Where it is merely tolerated, or operated in a negative cultural context of mistrust or suspicion, it may flounder. When embraced and celebrated, success is more likely. In Part Two we will turn to exploring what those elements of organizational culture and approach are that can enable flexibility in all its forms to flourish.

Challenges

So far, this chapter has explored a largely positive picture of flexible working. Future chapters will continue to look with more depth into the potential of flexible working to benefit inclusion and employee wellbeing. Although the benefits are many, this should not be taken to imply that operating flexible working is entirely without its challenges and issues – some of which are both significant and persistent. Flexible working challenges the default working model and not everyone will approve of this or be ready for its implications. As we shall explore later in the book, flexible working also brings with it challenges for managers, organizations and flexible workers themselves. Here are just a few of the key challenges experienced as a result of flexible forms of working.

Career progression

Some people believe that flexible working can be damaging for careers and evidence suggests that this fear is based in reality. Research by Chung (2018) found that 1 in 5 workers who use or have used flexible working arrangements have in the previous 12 months experienced some form of negative career consequence from doing so. According to research by flexible working company Timewise, 68 per cent of flexible workers accept compromises to their own career because they feel so grateful to have had their request accepted (Timewise, 2018). Part-time working in particular appears to be detrimental to both career progress and wage progression, offering restricted opportunities for promotion, with more junior part-time workers most likely to have no chance of progression at all (Jones, 2019).

Further research undertaken by Working Families (2017) asked parents why they did not seek flexible working arrangements. Some 12 per cent of fathers said it was because they feared being seen as less committed and 10 per cent said they believed it would hurt their career. Another 2017 survey found that 7 per cent of mothers felt that their career was suffering as a result of working flexibly (Workingmums, 2017).

Interestingly, however, the type of flexibility undertaken influences attitudes about the impact of flexible working. Where the form of flexibility involves working some form of reduced hours (part-time working), workers were 14 times more likely to have experienced negative career consequences than those who work flexibly but are still undertaking the equivalent of full-time work (such as flexi-time or part remote working). Remote working is perhaps not associated with such negative perceptions as it still aligns to the idea of the ideal worker who will uphold the 'work devotion schema' (Chung, 2018). In other words, we continue to value people who work long hours and who are (or appear to be) entirely committed to their work or organization over people who seek to balance work with other responsibilities or desires.

When we remember that it is predominantly women that undertake part-time work, mainly as a result of societal gender norms and the fact that women still undertake the majority of childcare and domestic labour, we can see here that, again, we have a critical inclusion issue. Women are more likely to work part-time, more likely to experience negative career consequences, less likely to be able to fulfil the role of the 'ideal worker' and more likely to face flexibility stigma from managers and colleagues. These issues are also bound up with organizational culture. The more a particular organization values and rewards the default, full-time model of work, and the more it conflates presence and performance, the greater these issues become for individuals working within them.

Altogether, this forms a bleak picture.

Work intensification

Several studies of flexible workers have raised concerns that flexible working arrangements can in some circumstances lead to work intensification, particularly in the case of those who work reduced hours (time flexibility) or remotely (location flexibility). It is easy to assume that flexible working will improve employee work–life balance, and for some people (as we shall see in Chapter 5 on flexible working and wellbeing) this is true – but it is not necessarily true of all situations or all employees. One of the many challenges of researching flexible working, or indeed seeking to find one consistent view of its impacts, benefits and issues, is the many different forms of flexibility that exist. These different forms can lead to varied outcomes, and identifying general statements is almost impossible; work intensification is just one example of this. Work intensification takes place when employees increase the effort that they put into their jobs, either by working harder or longer (the latter is sometimes referred to as 'extensification'). There are many factors that influence how hard or for how long employees work, some of which are cultural to the organization itself. According to research by Kelliher and Anderson from the University of Cranfield, flexible working can lead to work intensification; employees may feel that they have to work harder to somehow justify their working pattern or 'give back' to the organization in return for the flexibility provided, possibly through some sense of obligation. Workloads may not be sufficiently adjusted when employees reduce their working hours, and being away from the workplace (as with remote working) can make it easier to work harder or longer hours. Finally, those working fewer hours may simply have more energy to bring to their workplaces than those who typically work full-time as they are less tired (Kelliher and Anderson, 2010).

Flexible working stigma

Flexible working is associated with a range of stigma that can cause serious negative consequences for flexible workers. This stigma is interlinked with similar issues including the career stagnation point discussed above.

Research conducted by Chung (2018) examined flexibility stigma in detail, exploring perceptions that flexible workers were less committed or less productive than people working a standard pattern. In response to questions, 35 per cent of all workers agreed with the statement that those who work flexibly create more work for others and 32 per cent believed that those who worked flexibly had lower chances for promotion. These findings were highly gendered: more men were likely to discriminate against flexible workers and more women (particularly mothers) were likely to experience it. Additional research from the United States found similar issues around stigma, but also found that stigma varied along gender lines. This research found that employees who requested flexible working were perceived more negatively overall than those who did not request it and that those who requested location flexibility (for example, the ability to be able to work remotely or from home) were judged more negatively than those who requested time flexibility – perhaps because time-flexible workers are still more visible or present in the organization (Munsch, 2016). Perhaps even more interestingly, the same research found that employees who requested flexibility for childcare reasons were judged less negatively than those who requested it for other reasons (such as work–life balance), suggesting perhaps that some reasons for flexible working are perceived as somehow more legitimate or appropriate than others. The research also found worrying results in relation to the gender of the requester. Men who asked for flexible working were perceived as more likeable, respected and committed than women who made the same request. This was attributed to gender stereotypes in which men are afforded status from helping with childcare and domestic work in a way that women are not, as the latter is an expectation in the way that the former is not. From this research we can see just how prevalent stigma is within many organizations. Working flexibly can give rise to concerns (generally unsubstantiated) that flexible workers are somehow less committed or motivated than their non-flexible counterparts – as we will see in Chapter 6 discussing the myths of flexible working, there is no evidence to support these views, and in some cases evidence exists to demonstrate the exact opposite position. Despite this, stigma is a very real issue for flexible workers.

As we can see from the issues described here, as well as others that we will explore in later chapters, flexible working is not without its challenges. The complexity of the findings discussed here goes some way to show the challenges with flexible working research, as the different types of flexible working arrangements, who requests them and why, are all variables that lead to different outcomes. Some of these are related to deeply ingrained cultural and societal issues, as well as internal biases. However, every one of these challenges can be overcome – although doing so may neither be quick nor simple.

KEY TAKEAWAYS

There are many benefits that can result from flexible working, for organizations, managers and employees. Flexible working is not just a benefit for individual employees:

- Benefits can be found in relation to the attraction and retention of talent, organizational performance, employee engagement, sustainability, employee wellbeing and cost savings.
- There is a range of research and industry surveys that consistently supports these benefits of flexible forms of working.

- Flexible working does, however, bring with it a number of challenges for organizations, their managers and flexible workers themselves. Some of these challenges are in the form of myths and barriers. Others relate to organizational culture and broader societal norms. Generally, however, the benefits outweigh the challenges.

- Flexible working challenges include significant implications for flexible workers – organizations will need to ensure their strategies and approaches towards flexibility include plans for overcoming them.

- Whether flexible working is ultimately a benefit to individuals may depend on their specific working arrangement and the culture of the organization in which they undertake it.

- All organizations need to take talent management seriously – this includes how talent is attracted, retained, motivated, rewarded and engaged.

- Flexible working can support a range of talent-focused initiatives. It can act as a tool for talent acquisition, employee engagement, motivation and employee retention.

- There is still a lack of available flexible jobs in the labour market; flexible working can therefore act as a powerful lever to attract job applicants.

- Flexible working can form part of the employer brand – the overall positioning of the organization as a desirable employer.

References

Armstrong, A, Oliver, S and Wilkinson, S (2018) *Shades of Grey: An exploratory study of engagement in work teams*, Ashridge Executive Education

Atkinson, C and Hall, L (2011) Flexible working and happiness in the NHS, *Employee Relations*, Emerald Group Publishing

Chung, H (2018) Gender, flexibility stigma and the perceived negative consequences of flexible working in the UK, *Social Indicators Research*

CIPD (2016) *Employee Outlook, Employee Views on Working Life, focus on commuting and flexible working*, CIPD, London

CIPD (2019) *Megatrends: Flexible Working*, CIPD, London

Clarke, S and Holdsworth, L (2017) *Flexibility in the Workplace: Implications of flexible working arrangements for individuals, teams and organizations*, Acas

Deloitte (2019) *The Millennial Dad at Work*, in association with Daddilife, www.daddilife.com/wp-content/uploads/2019/05/The-Millenial-Dad-at-Work-Report-2019.pdf (archived at https://perma.cc/K8MV-NSSH)

De Menezes, L and Kelliher, C (2011) Flexible Working and Performance: A systematic review of the evidence for a business case, *International Journal of Management Reviews*

Dwelly, T and Lake, A (ed) (2008) *Can homeworking save the planet? How homes can become workspace in a low carbo economy'*, The Smith Institute

Gallup (2017) *State of the Global Workplace*, Gallup

International Workplace Group (2019) *Global Workplace Survey – Welcome to generation flex; the employee power shift*

IRS (2009) *Flexible working survey 2009, availability, take up and impact*, XpertHR, www.xperthr.co.uk/survey-analysis/irs-flexible-working-survey-2009-availability-take-up-and-impact/93627/ (archived at https://perma.cc/2HFU-6QN4)

Jones, L (2019) Women's Progression in the Workplace, Government Equalities Office, assets.publishing.service.gov.uk/government/uploads/system/uploads/attachment_data/file/840404/KCL_Main_Report.pdf (archived at https://perma.cc/8AJN-PTSS)

Kelliher, C and Anderson, D (2010) *Doing More With Less? Flexible working practices and the intensification of work*, The Tavistock Institute

Lyonette, C and Baldauf, B (2019) *Family Friendly Working Policies and Practices: Motivations, influences and impacts for employers*, Government Equalities Office

MacLeod, D and Clarke, N (2009) *Engaging for Success*, Department for Business, Innovation and Skills

Munsch, C (2016) *Flexible Work, Flexible Penalties: The effect of gender, childcare and type of request on flexibility bias*, Oxford University Press

Nanda, A (2019) *Work less to save the planet? How to make sure a four-day week actually cuts emissions*, The Conversation

NHS Inspiring Leaders Network (2019) *A National Survey of Healthcare Staff on Flexible Working*, The Inspiring Leaders Network and Yorkshire and The Humber Leadership Academy

Personnel Today (2018) New polls confirm desire for flexible working as 9 to 5 declines, www.personneltoday.com/hr/new-polls-confirm-desire-for-flexible-working-as-9-to-5-declines/ (archived at https://perma.cc/2NKS-VBDQ)

Pink, D (2018) *Drive: The surprising truth about what motivates us*, Canongate Books

Randstad (2016) *Employer branding: perception is reality*, International report

RSA (2013) *The Flex Factor: Realising the value of flexible working*, www.thersa.org/globalassets/pdfs/blogs/rsa_flex_report_15072013.pdf (archived at https://perma.cc/V4SA-MLMT)

Smeaton, D, Ray, K and Knight, G (2014) *Costs and Benefits to Businesses of Adopting Work Life Balance Practices: A literature review*, Department for Business, Innovation and Skills

Timewise (2018) *Part time work: the exclusion zone*, timewise.co.uk/wp-content/uploads/2018/09/Part-Time_Work_Exclusion_Zone.pdf (archived at https://perma.cc/8NGL-YNVG)

Timewise (2019) *Flexible Working: A talent imperative*, timewise.co.uk/wp-content/uploads/2019/06/Flexible_working_Talent_Imperative.pdf (archived at https://perma.cc/M6W2-7EWG)

Wheatley, D (2017) Employee satisfaction and use of flexible working arrangements, *Work, Employment and Society*, University of Birmingham

Working Families/Cranfield School of Management (2009) *Flexible Working and Performance, Summary of Research*, Working Families

Working Families (2017) *Modern Families Index*, workingfamilies.org.uk/wp-content/uploads/2017/01/MFI_2017_Report_UK_FINAL_web-1.pdf (archived at https://perma.cc/74X4-HW4X)

Working Families (2018) *Top employers for working families benchmark report 2018*, Working Families

WorkHuman (2019) *The Future of Work is Human: International employee survey report 2019*, Workhuman Analytics and Research Institute

Workingmums (2017) *Annual Survey 2017*, www.workingmums.co.uk/workingmums-annual-survey-2017/ (archived at https://perma.cc/8J7C-N2JG)

Workplace Insight (2019) *Working Mums Call For More Flexible Work Options*, workplaceinsight.net/working-mums-call-for-more-flexible-work-options/ (archived at https://perma.cc/XE37-QKEF)

XpertHR (2018) /*Flexible Working Policies and Practice Survey 2018*, XpertHR

03

Flexible working and the future of work

As discussed in the Introduction, flexible working can be understood through several lenses. First of all there is the individualistic view that flexible working is a process through which employees can access alternative forms of working, primarily benefiting the individual applicant. This is both a fairly limited as well as a limiting view of flexibility, and if we compare it with the data discussed in Chapter 2, we find it ignores many of the wider benefits that it can deliver.

Flexible working also has a much broader context relating to both relatively recent changes to ways in which we work today, as well as predictions for the future of work. Indeed, it has been suggested that in the future, flexible working will be the norm rather than the exception (Chung and van der Lippe, 2018), although whether this prediction turns out to be valid remains to be seen. For it to do so would require a significant shift in current attitudes and working practices.

This chapter will explore current workplace trends and predictions for the future of the workplace, drawing on the work of leading thinkers on the subject, and will set flexible working in the context of the future of work. The factors that influence the future of work are many and interrelated, as well as hard to predict over the longer term. When we look back over recent decades and even centuries, we can see a picture of constant workplace change and development. The key difference between the past and today is the sheer speed of that progress.

Before we begin to look forward to the future, let us turn for a moment to consider the past. The late 18th and the 19th centuries were periods of significant economic and social change across much of the developed world. The very nature of work was fundamentally changed. Prior to this time many people were engaged in work activities either within or very close to their homes. A whole range of factors came together to entirely alter this picture. New methods of production, better modes of travel, innovations in machinery and new ways to communicate are just some of the changes that enabled this period of rapid transformation that we now know as the Industrial Revolution.

The Industrial Revolution was characterized by the rise of large factories, workers moving closer to cities to take advantage of new work opportunities and increased mechanization as opposed to traditional methods of hand production taking place in the home or local village. In some cases it also led to poor working and living conditions for many workers. In making this transition to the factory, many workers gave up the autonomy of working for themselves to answer to the company clock and we saw the emergence of work taking place at the same time and at the same place – the default model of work was born.

That process of mechanization and increasing technology continued at pace, and so did the impacts upon society, individuals and the economy. Fast-forwarding to more recent times, the last few decades of working life have been a picture of significant disruption; in the world of work there is no such thing as the status quo (and perhaps never has been). A mere 30 years ago, the UK economy was dominated by manufacturing and primary industries such as coal-mining, car production and steelwork. Trade union membership was high, the 'job for life' commonplace, and most people retired at 65 – if not considerably earlier. Jump to the present day and we find an entirely different picture. Many of those primary industries barely exist, manufacturing has drastically declined, the demographics of our workplaces have changed significantly, trade union membership continues to fall, the service industry dominates and job tenure is ever shorter. Technology has replaced many jobs and new jobs have taken their place.

Workplaces are technology filled. More and more of the world is connected by mobile device, social media appears to be everywhere and a significant proportion of the population has a smartphone. We are beginning to see the influence and potential of artificial intelligence, cognitive assistants and virtual reality – although it is very clear that we are only at the beginning of this particular journey. Change is indeed constant – and flexible working is just one part of this evolution. This means that flexible working can perhaps be seen through one further lens: a rejection of the old ways, of what began at the turn of the Industrial Revolution, and a return to the autonomy of the distant past.

However we choose to view the future of work, there is no question that all organizations will need to adapt, as will the people who work for them.

The big trends

There has been a great deal written about the future of work and just how it may evolve, and many theories and perspectives have been proposed. Predicting the future is no easy task and we should be cautious about making too many predictions. There are, however, some common themes arising from within the various theories and perspectives. These themes include the impact of the ever-increasing capability of technology, the automation of jobs, changing workforce demographics, globalization and the need for an increasing focus on corporate social responsibility and the environment. Flexible working is a thread that winds through these themes. To meet these challenges organizations will need to be focused on the future, alert to new trends and agile in the way that they undertake their business. They will need to be flexible, too.

Changing demographics and multiple generations

Recent years have seen a shift in the demographics of the workforce, a trend that we can expect to continue into the future. As well as the increasing number of women in the workplace, this demographic shift is driven partly by the fact that people are living – and therefore choosing to work – longer. This in turn means that there are now more generations in the workforce simultaneously than ever before. There has been a great deal written about generational differences and the recent generations that have entered into the workforce in the last decade or so (often referred to as Generation Y, Generation X or Millennials). Much of this commentary is highly generalized, but there is some evidence to suggest that these employees are seeking a different deal to the one their parents settled for, including more flexibility in the work that they do and how they do it (Hot Spot Movement, 2012).

Only a few decades ago, the average employee would not have lived long past the typical retirement age, but many people can now expect to live well into their late 70s or 80s. Living to 100 is becoming commonplace – in fact, figures indicate that 1 in 3 babies born in the UK today will live to see their one-hundredth birthday (ONS, 2016). Longer life expectancy has significant implications for individuals, society and organizations. Futurologists fore-cast that it will lead to fundamental shifts in the way that we live our lives and how we work.

One of the immediate practical implications is that employees will not necessarily want to retire in their mid-sixties as is often the case in the default model of work. They may want to retire later or find other ways of retaining the necessary income to fund a much longer life. There are real potential business benefits of permitting – or even encouraging – them to do so. Retaining older workers can help organizations to keep their valuable knowledge, experience and skills for longer, as well as increase the diversity of their workforce.

Flexible working can be a realistic alternative to full retirement and can support the attraction and retention of older workers, especially as there is clear evidence that they have a desire to do so. As we have already seen, whilst the stereotype of someone who wants flexible working is a parent (often the mother of a small child), the desire to work flexibly appears to cut across all age groups. According to a 2019 survey, younger people (18–34) are the most likely to want to work flexibly, at 92 per cent. Amongst full-time workers, 88 per cent of 35- to 54-year-olds and 72 per cent of those aged 55+ want to work flexibly (Timewise, 2019). Flexible working there-fore is part of the solution to attracting these workers (and younger ones too).

The 100-year life has other, potentially far-reaching implications for working arrangements, and the default working model in particular. Leading business futurologist Lynda Gratton theorizes that longer lives will lead to major shifts in how we work and live. Today, many of us experience a famil-iar three-phase life that comprises full-time education, work and retirement, all of which are undertaken in a mostly linear fashion at typical life stages. For example, if you ask someone to think of the average undergraduate, most people will think of someone in their late teens or early twenties rather than someone of middle age. Gratton believes that these traditional life stages will be significantly disrupted. She believes that people simply will not want to work full-time, in one career, for 50 years, and we will see patterns of work emerging that are beyond those that are the primary focus of this book, the straightforward flexible working arrangement. Instead we may see entirely new trends emerge, such as multiple career paths, people taking regular career breaks or time out of the workforce, perhaps returning to education at later life stages or as they need to develop new types of skills to meet the demands of a changing labour market (Gratton and Scott, 2017).

Flexible working has a role to play here too. Employees who are going to be working for more than 50 years may not want to be tied to the full-time, 9 to 5 model for this duration. Flexible working can support people through these different life stages, whilst they retrain, take some time out of this longer working life or as they approach retirement.

The Introduction to this book argued that flexible working in its broadest sense was about fundamentally rethinking how we work, and empowering people to work how, where and when they work best. A longer working life may encourage more people than ever before to work differently to the way we have done in past decades.

Technology

Recent decades have seen astonishing leaps in technology capability, and this has been the driver of a great change relating to how we live and work. It has helped to open up whole new markets for business, consumers and talent alike. New products and services have emerged as a result: consider household names such as Uber, Deliveroo, Tinder, TripAdvisor, Netflix and Airbnb. Each of these provides services that simply did not exist just a few years ago – and could not have done so. Through the smart devices in our pockets we track our physical activity, navigate around the city, do our banking and the weekly shopping and listen to music. We network, share photographs, rate products and services and undertake learning. We are constantly connected. Technology has also fundamentally changed the way that we communicate through the continued rise of social media and ever cheaper and faster ways of connecting people. Cloud technology is now ubiquitous and there are millions of people connected across the world via mobile devices.

There is no doubt that technology itself is a key enabler of flexible working. Technology has connected us easily and cheaply with colleagues and customers all over the world. Many workers today are entirely effective at any time and in any location, purely via a wifi connection. Fewer employees therefore need to be bound to the default working model if they do not wish to be – and as we shall see when we talk about globalization, this may no longer be what organizations need either if they are to serve the global markets that technology enables. Forms of working have recently become possible that would have been completely impossible a decade ago. This assumes, of course, that employees have access to both the necessary software and hardware to do so. According to the Royal Society of Arts, just over half of employees are still doing most of their work on an employer-provided desktop which removes their ability to be location flexible unless they are prepared to fill the gap with their own devices – if that is even permitted or possible on the corporate network (RSA, 2013). If organizations are to realize some of the benefits of the future of work through flexible working, it is clear that they will also need to invest in the necessary technology infrastructure to enable them to do so.

Unfortunately, many workplaces do not harness the technology that is already available to them, preferring to stick to tried and tested methods and 'the way we have always done it'. Those who are now in senior leadership positions in many organizations entered the workforce before much of the technology we now take for granted was in regular use. They may have worked in the same way for decades – it is this generation and the one before it that created many of the ways of working that we are currently familiar with. Although on the face of it, it may look like we have introduced technology into our workplaces, we have not really updated the way that we work to make full use of it; instead, we have simply incorporated technology into the old approaches. Consider university lecturing as an example. Teaching is based on the idea that an expert shares his or her knowledge and learning with others. Lecturers design assignments, help students expand their learning through discussion and reflection, give lectures and hold seminars. Many lecturers (and indeed teachers in all levels of education) have begun to use technology. Some of them may teach using iPads, incorporate online discussion, set blogs rather than essays as a method for assessment. However, the primary format of content delivery remains face to face and has not changed at all – an expert at the front of the room for whom all have gathered. The same could be said of workplace processes.

There is plenty of available technology that can support flexible (and particularly remote) forms of working. The good news is that some of it is entirely free to use (although as is often the case with software, there is a free version and a paid-for version with enhanced features). For simple video- or web-conferencing there are apps such as Skype, Zoom and GoToMeeting that allow employees to meet virtually from wherever they are working. Enterprise social networks are company-specific online social media networks that support internal communication; examples include Yammer and Workplace. Collaboration platforms like Slack or Microsoft Teams allow colleagues to share information, upload files and organize discussions – with the added bonus of reducing email traffic. Files can be saved in the cloud, providing access anywhere and any when, and are easily shared with others through applications like SharePoint and Dropbox. Other applications will allow for instant messaging, screen-sharing, video chats, teleconferences, meeting scheduling and the forwarding of phone calls to anywhere.

All too often, organizations are not using the full capability of the IT resources they already have. This is a much bigger issue than simply its impact upon flexible working. Although the future is hard to predict, what we do know is that the capability of technology will continue to grow. It will continue to have the potential to change how we live, work, socialize, do business. Fears will continue on an individual level (what does this mean for me?), at a societal level (will the robots take all the jobs?) and at an organizational one – generally in terms of how to respond. There are no quick or simple answers to be found.

For the purposes of this book, we will turn to the issue of technology again in Part Two, and identify the practical issues to address to ensure that technology is understood and used to enable successful flexible working.

There is one thing of which we can be certain: technology will only continue to develop, speed up and integrate with every aspect of our lives.

Globalization

The world is not of course getting smaller – but it does sometimes feel that way. A couple of generations ago, international travel was neither possible nor affordable for the vast majority of people. Communicating globally was equally difficult and expensive. Today it is routine, perhaps even mundane.

Over the last 30 years, global trade has increased at a rapid level, largely enabled by the forms of technology we have just discussed. Internet, email, mobile devices and social media have removed many of the old barriers, allowing organizations to operate globally and on a 24/7 basis. Technology and globalization are interlinked. It is technology that has shaped these new ways to work, communicate and do business, and increasing globalization leads to even further demands for better technology. Once again, we see a future of work trend as both an enabler of and driver for flexible forms of working.

Where teams are distributed and increasingly virtual in order to serve virtual markets, flexible working becomes an essential requirement rather than a nice to have. If we can work anywhere, we can also potentially live anywhere too. For the global organization, flexible working arrangements can be used to allow employees to work across locations and time zones, and allow businesses to serve new markets and a whole new customer base. Talent acquisition becomes global too. No longer is an organization bound by geographical constraints and who might be prepared to undertake the commute to its head office; it can search for and accommodate employee talent anywhere, as long as those individuals have access to the necessary technology to enable them to do their work. The labour market becomes truly global. Of course, globalization is not the only reason that organizations may need employees to work outside of the default model. Consumers are rarely content to engage and buy from businesses that are only open 9 to 5 either. We are a truly 24/7 society.

For many people, the idea of truly working from anywhere, entirely untethered from an office environment, completely empowered to work on their own schedule, is a distant dream – the preserve of the lucky few. There are, however, organizations where this is happening. Automatic, the owner of blogging platforms WordPress and Tumblr does just this. They own no real estate and have no offices. Their employees can be based anywhere in the world, have no fixed schedules and work in teams that are entirely dispersed, often not even in the same countries or time zones. People do not meet face to face and they communicate almost entirely via technology (Berkun, 2013). This is the ultimate form of flexibility; employees entirely empowered to work in the way that works best for them whilst still achieving organizational goals. Suggest such an approach to many organizations, however, and it would be rejected outright, and reason after reason why it just would not work for them would be offered. This model will not work for all organizations, but for Automatic, it fits their particular context.

Today, the demand for flexible working is often addressed on a case-by-case basis as a response to an individual request. Each request is considered individually, with reference to the immediate operational situation, with employees being accommodated where possible – or where attitudes permit. This approach is only sustainable to a point. If the demand for flexibility is as significant as surveys suggest, this indicates that a much broader approach is required by organizations. Some of the ideas discussed in this chapter are not yet mainstream; they represent a probable future, but one in which flexibility is key. This future demands that flexibility needs to be tackled at scale, and centred in the future of work and workplaces.

There is one final and very fundamental issue to consider about the future: climate change. The risks to our planet are well documented and very real. The environment is the responsibility of each of us: individuals, governments, organizations. We have already discussed the issue of sustainability in Chapter 2. There are no easy solutions to the problems that face us, and there is no single solution, just concerted action across many areas. Social responsibility is likely to continue to rise up the organizational agenda and there is much that business can do. Flexible working can perhaps be just one small step that will contribute in some way to this significant challenge. As employees and consumers become more discerning and more demanding in the choices they make about the organizations that they work and purchase from, the business case for corporate responsibility will be made in addition to the moral and social one.

When these future trends of technology, globalization and demographic change come together a very different, very flexible future is within reach. Flexibility is the golden thread that runs through them all. Here is an example from one global organization, utilizing flexibility to achieve its business aims.

CASE STUDY
Thales

Global organization Thales works across industries including transportation, defence, security and aerospace. They employ over 6,500 in the UK and are strong advocates for flexible working, evidenced by their overall approach and feedback from their employees. In their 2019 employee survey, employees were asked to reflect on their work–life balance; 95 per cent of the respondents said 'my working arrangements are flexible enough to meet my personal needs' with an overall 91 per cent favourable response when asked about their work–life blend.

Thales offer a range of flexible working options including flexible hours around informal core hours, nine-day fortnights, compressed hours, phased retirement, four-day week (with full pay) and a half-day Friday (where employees work four days at eight hours and one at five). They have seen a particular increase in the nine-day fortnight across the organization including at director level – senior leaders visibly work flexibly. Employees can also work from home on an informal basis. Employees are empowered to work in the way that suits them and their work and life circumstances. This ranges from employees who are managing childcare responsibilities to those who want to pursue a hobby or interest.

Talent is a major business driver behind the Thales approach. Flexible working is seen as a way to address skills shortages and increasing competition for talent (including competing for talent against competitors who already offered more flexible working opportunities) and to improve diversity in a traditionally male-dominated industry. It is also about recognizing employee demand: their employees asked for flexibility and Thales was keen to meet those expectations.

As a result of flexible working, Thales have seen increased employee retention, employee satisfaction and productivity, as well as received anecdotal evidence from employees that they have chosen to work with Thales as a result of their flexible working offering. Through internal surveys employees have commented that they feel trusted and that Thales is truly committed to supporting their work–life balance. Many employees are required by the nature of their work to book their working time to projects meaning that there is a clear line of sight between utilization and productivity and the business can clearly demonstrate the link to flexible working. This evidence has been central to winning over those who were initially sceptical about flexible working.

Thales have introduced tools to better support remote working including an internal video/chat facility on each laptop, allowing employees to join meetings whilst working remotely or from home. As a global business, there can be a requirement for employees to join meetings outside of their 'normal' working hours, depending on time zones. Where they do so, or when they travel globally, employees are encouraged to take this time back at a later date. The technology supports this business need for flexibility from employees.

Although there is a formal policy on flexible working, much of what happens in practice is informal and takes place at a team level. Internal SMART Charters are put in place by teams, which form their local agreement about ways of working, including location, timing of meetings and how they will share information between themselves. Thales is an example of an organization that has embraced the future of work through the provision of flexibility.

KEY TAKEAWAYS

- There are several big trends influencing the future of work, including: increasing technology, globalization, changing workplace demographics and an urgent need to consider corporate social responsibility and ethical business models.

- Flexible working is at the heart of the future of work. These current and future workplace trends both enable flexible working and are drivers for its introduction.

- All organizations will need to respond to these current and future trends, or risk being left behind by their competitors or losing out on talent.

- Flexible working can be considered on a case-by-case basis on receipt of a request – but organizations will reap the benefits of flexible working when adopting a strategic approach, taking into account the implications of the future of work.

- Adapting to the future of work is not just the responsibility of organizations. Employees will also need to think about their own response, especially in terms of developing their skills and planning for a longer life.

- The future is uncertain, and the world of work will continue to change and develop at pace. True flexibility therefore includes the ability to constantly adapt – and so therefore must an organization's approach to flexible working.

References

Berkun, S (2013) *The Year Without Pants: WordPress and the future of work*, John Wiley and Sons

Chung, H and van der Lippe, T (2018) Flexible working: Work life balance and gender equality, *Social Indicators Research*, doi.org/10.1007/s11205-018-2025-x (archived at https://perma.cc/78H2-YT94)

Gratton, L and Scott, A (2017) *The 100-Year Life: Living and working in an age of longevity*, Bloomsbury Business, London

Hot Spot Movement (2012) *The Benefits of Flexible Working Arrangements: A future of work report*, The Future of Work Institute, www.bc.edu/content/dam/files/centers/cwf/individuals/pdf/benefitsCEOFlex.pdf (archived at https://perma.cc/NP4X-BG5U)

ONS (2016) *What are your chances of living to 100?*, Office for National Statistics, www.ons.gov.uk/peoplepopulationandcommunity/birthsdeathsandmarriages/lifeexpectancies/articles/whatareyourchancesoflivingto100/2016-01-14 (archived at https://perma.cc/QH6W-2F8X)

RSA (2013) *The Flex Factor: Realizing the value of flexible working*, www.thersa.org/globalassets/pdfs/blogs/rsa_flex_report_15072013.pdf (archived at https://perma.cc/V4SA-MLMT)

Timewise (2019) *Flexible Working: A talent imperative*, timewise.co.uk/wp-content/uploads/2019/06/Flexible_working_Talent_Imperative.pdf (archived at https://perma.cc/M6W2-7EWG)

04

Flexible working and inclusion

The rationale for flexible working is all too often focused on benefits for working parents. Although this group can undoubtedly benefit significantly from flexible working arrangements – a 2019 survey by campaign group Pregnant then Screwed, for example, found that the high cost of childcare causes anxiety for 84 per cent of households with almost 1 in 5 working parents giving up their jobs as a result (Workingmums, 2019) – there are wider benefits for equality, diversity and inclusion that can result from a greater focus on workplace flexibility. Many people, for many reasons, are unable to engage in the default model of full-time, Monday to Friday, 9 to 5 work, leaving them excluded from the labour market. There are specific challenges for these employees that can be addressed through the introduction of flexible working.

Although often used interchangeably, the terms equality, diversity and inclusion have different meanings. Whilst *equal opportunity* is primarily about ensuring that individuals are not treated differently or discriminated against (in a legal context), it is in many ways an approach which prioritizes compliance. *Diversity* is about recognizing difference, but not necessarily leveraging it to drive organizational success. *Inclusion* is a much broader term.

According to the Chartered Institute of Personnel and Development (CIPD), inclusion can be defined as an approach where difference is seen as a benefit, and where perspectives and differences are shared resulting in better decisions. An inclusive working environment is one in which everyone feels valued, that their contribution matters and they are able to perform to their full potential, no matter what their background, identity or circumstances. An inclusive workplace enables a diverse range of people to work together effectively (CIPD, 2019a). Everyone benefits from inclusion: the employee, the organization and society in general.

This chapter will consider the specific, positive impacts on equality, diversity and inclusion beyond working parents, where organizations embrace flexible working arrangements.

Gender

Issues of gender and flexible working are inextricably linked. Whilst flexible working is legally available to any employee in the UK, it can hardly be described as gender neutral. Men and women experience different outcomes from working flexibly and different gender norms apply. Chung and van der Lippe (2018) argue that you cannot really understand the consequences of flexible working without considering the importance of gender and the different ways that men and women use flexible working arrangements.

It is often (incorrectly) assumed that flexible working is desired predominantly by women after they have had a family or taken maternity leave, even though the evidence points to a much wider desire from a whole range of employees to work flexibly. As we have already discussed, some forms of flexible working (such as part-time working) are dominated by women: the UK has one of the highest proportions of female part-time workers as a share of the female working population in the whole of the EU (Jones, 2019). It does not, however, follow that this is because women want to work part-time, but is part of a wider mix of complex societal factors. When a typical so-called 'nuclear' family decides that one person will reduce their hours or seek flexibility, it often falls to the woman in the relationship because it is more socially acceptable to make such a request and she is more likely to earn less than a male partner as a result of the gender pay gap (a subject to which we will return shortly). She will often then find herself earning less, or her career curtailed, and thus the gap is further perpetuated. There is also the issue of reliable, affordable childcare – another contributing factor to the move towards part-time work. Finally, there is the incompatibility of the default model of work and the school timetable, where both children and employees are expected to start at (approximately) 9am. Where working arrangements are inflexible, this can leave parents (and women in particular) with a choice between part-time work or expensive wrap-around care.

Part-time working is associated with shutting down pay progression for women and this is a key reason why the gender pay gap exists, and continues to be perpetuated. This is not just a UK issue. Evidence from across

Europe points to similar issues; female dominated workplaces not only have lower wages but also worse working conditions (Chung, 2019a).

Part-time working is a form of flexible working and this is a book that advocates flexibility – but it also advocates choice. Whilst flexibility itself is a good thing, forced flexible working (in the sense that it is all that is available and practical for a family but then results in poor outcomes for those undertaking it) is not. As discussed in the Introduction, when some people think of flexibility they think only of forms of reduced-hours working and we know that this can lead to negative consequences for individuals.

It is not just part-time jobs that bring with them gender-related challenges when it comes to flexible working arrangements. As we discussed in Chapter 2, women who seek to work flexibly in order to fulfil childcare commitments experience both career stagnation and various forms of stigma. Female workers have been described as experiencing a 'motherhood penalty' – in which women with children suffer from systematic discrimination in a multitude of ways, including the gender pay gap (Munsch, 2016).

These are issues both for the individual woman, but also for our wider society. It is estimated that the under-utilization of women's skills costs the UK economy between 1.3 and 2 per cent of GDP every year (Women and Equalities Committee, 2016).

According to the Government Equalities Office, greater access to flexible working arrangements could be the key to women's retention and progression in the workplace, and gender equality across society as a whole (Jones, 2019). For example, evidence suggests that flexible working can help women stay in employment after the birth of their first child as well as decrease the likelihood that they will reduce their working hours after the first or any subsequent childbirth (Chung and van der Horst, 2017). It is easy to see increased flexible working as a potential solution to achieving greater gender equality in the workplace – although the range and complexity of factors that lead to gender inequality do not give rise to easy solutions. There is much that flexible working can do, but there are risks associated with it too.

There is a counter argument that says flexible working can also reinforce gender roles and gender inequality. This unintended consequence can arise from men working longer hours as a result of flexible working arrangements and women increasing their care duties (Chung, 2019b). The idea of women fulfilling childcare and other caring responsibilities fits neatly with gender stereotypes, whilst their male partner works full-time and longer hours and is the main earner (Fagan *et al*, 2006). Therefore, rather than flexible working driving changes in society and gender norms, it simply leads to more of the same. Those stereotypes are challenged when more men work flexibly – and this is something we know that many men do want.

When it comes to the outcomes of flexible working, it appears that there are good forms and bad forms – and there are gender issues at play here too. 'Good' flexibility is flexibility that predominantly benefits the organization. Examples include working from home (allows for longer working hours, being constantly connected) and whilst not exactly a form of flexible working as described typically in this book, leavism (working whilst on holiday or other forms of leave). Less good flexibility is that typically undertaken by mothers or carers (also often women), such as forms of reduced-hours working or working patterns that enable non-work-related activities. This is another example of where flexible working, which has the potential to deliver so many benefits, actually leads to unintended and negative consequences. Managers may look to the form of flexibility undertaken and use this to form decisions about how committed someone is to their work and the organization itself, having potential career penalties for those undertaking them (Leslie *et al*, 2012).

Right now, flexible forms of working may enable caring or work–life balance, but do not offer parity around pay (which we will explore shortly), progression and experience. Quality flexible working is too rare, part-time work is underpaid and leads to career stagnation and there is a poor perception in general about flexible workers. If these issues are to be comprehensively addressed, the flexible working revolution also demands a fundamental revolution in underlying organizational culture and individual attitudes. Until we can reframe the conflation between the default model of work and career success, the potential of flexible working will be unrealized. Today, flexible working is part of the solution for achieving gender equality in the workplace – unfortunately, it also remains, for now at least, part of the problem.

Gender pay gap

The gender pay gap measures the difference between the hourly pay (based on median earnings) of the average male worker and the average female worker. It is not the same as equal pay, which considers whether men and women are being paid the same amount for the same work, or work of equivalent value. Since 2018, UK companies with more than 250 employees have been required by law to publish their gender pay gap on an annual basis: this legislation is part of a series of measures aiming to reduce the gap. The causes of the gender pay gap are complex and interrelated – and not all of it can be properly explained.

The current gender pay gap in the UK is 8.9 per cent for full-time employees. When all employees are taken into account the gap stands at 17.3 per cent. The difference between full-time and all employees is largely attributed to the fact that women undertake significantly more part-time jobs which tend to have lower hourly median pay than full-time jobs, and are more likely to be in lower-paid occupations in general (ONS, 2019). Women also work part-time because they are also undertaking a disproportionate amount of unpaid caring responsibilities (Women and Equalities Committee, 2016). These figures show a slight decline from the previous year, but overall there is slow progress in terms of reducing the pay gap between men and women. What we do not really know from the data that we have is how many women are working part-time because they want or need to, and how many are working part-time because that is the only work they are able to find.

The gender pay gap really begins to widen when women become parents. Prior to this, the gaps between men and women are small. Following the birth of a first child, there is barely any difference to men's working patterns, whereas women's are significantly impacted as they shift towards (often) part-time work – work that has been said to shut down wage progress (Jones, 2019). Time out of the labour market for maternity leave can set back women's careers and they fall behind male counterparts. Sometimes women have moved into part-time work because they feel like they have no choice but to do so or because of the lack of available and affordable childcare.

The Women and Equalities Committee has referred to part-time working as 'career death', in part because it is often lower paid – the so-called 'part-time pay penalty'. However, it is not just part-time work that is low paid: work that is traditionally female dominated (such as care work) is also often low-paid work, partly because it is less valued than occupations more dominated by men. The Women and Equalities Committee also point to gendered education choices, occupational 'downgrading' (women working beneath their capabilities in lower-paid jobs due to the lack of flexible or part-time senior roles and career paths), and, finally, direct and indirect discrimination (2016).

In recent years, successive UK governments have taken a number of steps to reduce the size of the gender pay gap including encouraging more women on boards, increasing the amount of free childcare and improving careers advice for girls. The 2014 extension of flexible working to all employees with 26 weeks' service, discussed in the Introduction, was one action that aimed to reduce the size of the UK gender pay gap (Women and Equalities Committee, 2016).

Flexible working clearly has a role to play in the reduction of the gender pay gap. For example, more and better quality part-time or job-share opportunities at senior levels will lead to higher pay and reduce career stagnation. Of course, as we have already seen, there is much more to flexible working than forms of reduced hours, and many of these forms of flexibility such as compressed hours, homeworking or staggered hours (currently somewhat less popular in the UK labour market) can also help women (on whom the burden so often falls) to balance their career and home responsibilities.

Encouraging more fathers to take up the opportunity for flexible working is also seen as having an important role in the reduction of the gender pay gap. This starts with parental leave (Chung, 2018). Under current UK legislation, fathers are entitled to take two weeks' paid paternity leave (at statutory rates unless the employer in question chooses to enhance the amount) following the birth or adoption of a child. In addition, all parents of children under the age of five are entitled to up to four weeks' unpaid leave per annum, per child. Shared Parental Leave (SPL), the ability for both parents to share a year's leave after the birth of a child, was introduced in the UK in 2014. Some of these rights require a particular length of service and are not available to self-employed workers. Take-up of SPL is extremely low. For the father to take some of the leave also requires the mother to give up some of hers, which not all women will want to do. This can be compared to the approach in Sweden where fathers have a right to 90 days entirely separately to the leave entitlement of their partner.

When more men across society in general take a greater involvement with childcare and work flexibly, this will not only support the reduction of the gender pay gap but also help to challenge the stigma of flexible working – and in particular its framing as a 'mother's' issue.

There is another type of gap that is relevant to gender and pay – the gender commuting gap. This is the gap that exists between the average commutes of male and female workers. Recent research from the Office for National Statistics suggests that UK men commute for longer than women, and that just like the gender pay gap itself, this gap begins to widen after the birth of a family's first child and continues to grow for the decade to follow (2018b). Men undertake almost two-thirds of commutes lasting more than an hour and are more likely to commute by train. In contrast, women are more likely to live close to their place of work (ONS, 2018b). What we do not know from this data is how much of this relates to personal choice and the availability of work, and how much relates to decisions and societal factors that are also causal factors for the gender pay gap – for example, women undertaking the bulk of domestic responsibilities (such as school drop-off or pick-up) and therefore needing to work close to home to facilitate this. This issue highlights how interrelated many of the factors influencing gender and pay are, but also how flexible working can make a positive impact. If home-working and flexible-schedule forms of flexibility were more available and acceptable, fewer decisions of this nature would be required in families and couples.

Fathers and flexible working

Although this book seeks to argue that there is more to flexible working than simply supporting working parents, there are specific inclusion issues that relate to fathers. We know that in many households, after having children it is women who undertake the bulk of childcare and domestic labour and it is often women that work part-time after having children. This can lead to what is described as the '1.5 household work model'; the father is working full-time and the mother part-time (Fagan *et al*, 2006). Whilst this still may be the norm, this is not necessarily what fathers (or their partners) desire. According to Working Families, a huge 82 per cent of fathers who work full-time said that they would like to spend more time with their family (Working Families, 2011). The introduction of SPL in the UK in 2014 was supposed to start to level the playing field, and help fathers take a more active role with their families. Take-up has, however, been notoriously low, as we discussed in the previous section. Where many employers enhance maternity leave, not all of them have chosen to similarly improve internal policies from the statutory minimum obligation.

In 2019, Deloitte undertook a survey into the Millennial father and his experiences of being a working parent. This survey found that:

- one-third of fathers surveyed reported having already left a job for one which will allow them to spend more time with their children;

- a further one-third of fathers were currently looking to do just the same;
- only 1 in 5 of those who requested flexible working had their request approved;
- one-third of fathers experience tension when needing time off to attend appointments or illnesses;
- the tension felt by fathers does not just come from the organization itself (and its managers) but colleagues too;
- some 37 per cent of fathers say that they have experienced negative impacts on their mental health as a result of trying to balance work and being a parent;
- guilt is a prominent emotion for fathers – guilt with line managers, partners, children, about colleagues (Deloitte, 2019).

Some of these experiences will be very familiar to working mothers. Men can also find themselves experiencing a particular form of flexible-working stigma that has been referred to as 'femininity stigma' which arises when men step outside the traditional image of the male as a breadwinner and engage with caring responsibilities (Chung, 2018).

Encouraging more fathers to work flexibly as well as undertaking forms of family leave such as SPL can have a range of benefits. As discussed previously, SPL is not just about encouraging fathers to spend more time with their children – it can also support the reduction of the gender pay gap. We know that women workers experience flexible working stigma, as well as other forms of work-related discrimination and bias. There are some employers who are reluctant to hire women in the first place, fearing the costs associated with maternity leave, or are unwilling to promote them for the same reasons. These are the same employers who are possibly unlikely to welcome flexible working requests too. However, when it is just as likely that men will take a period of leave or seek to work in a way that enables them to balance work and family, this source of discrimination and stereotyping is tackled at source. Traditional gender roles are challenged rather than perpetuated. It also begins to chip away at our prevalent long-hours cultures and presenteeism.

Individual fathers themselves can experience the personal benefits associated with improved work–life balance and spending more time with their children. Where flexible working and participation in childcare is seen as gender neutral, everyone can benefit – men, women, children and society.

Employees with disabilities

Employees with disabilities experience numerous disadvantages both in the workplace and whilst seeking work opportunities. Nearly 1 in 5 of the UK population between the ages of 16 and 64 are disabled. In 2018, of disabled people aged 16–64 years, 50.9 per cent were in employment, whilst 80.7 per cent of non-disabled people were in employment. Disabled employees typically earn less than their non-disabled colleagues. In 2018 that pay gap was just over 12 per cent – a figure that has barely moved in the last five years (ONS, 2018a). Disabled employees can find themselves beset by a range of stereotyped or outdated views including employers who are concerned about the costs of employing someone with disabilities, or assumptions that disability might also equate to high levels of sickness absence.

From an entirely practical point of view, commuting to and from work can be a particular challenge for those with physical disabilities. The accessibility and overcrowding of public transport can present a very specific barrier to working in its own right, excluding some employees from being able to travel to potential workplaces at all, or during peak times. Also depending on the particular nature of their condition or health, some employees with disabilities may not be able to work full-time. It is easy to see that flexible working can therefore be a potential solution to address some of these more practical challenges, which in turn can support change in more structural and systemic issues.

Disability is a protected characteristic under the Equality Act 2010. Under this legislation employers have a number of legal duties, including the requirement to make reasonable adjustments for employees (or potential employees) with a disability. For the purposes of the Act, a disability is a physical or mental health condition that has a substantial and long-term impact on an individual's ability to undertake normal day-to-day activities. What amounts to a reasonable adjustment will vary according to the circumstances, and the size and resources of the organization are relevant to the subject of reasonableness. Flexible working can amount to a potential reasonable adjustment under the legislation in some circumstances. Many of the forms of flexible working discussed in Chapter 1 could support a disabled worker and help them to continue to work in an effective way, participating in a labour market that they might otherwise find difficult to access. Homeworking in particular can be an adjustment that reduces the need to commute. Other adjustments that might also amount to flexible working can include reduced working hours, or amended start and finish times (to avoid peak commuting times).

A small number of conditions such as cancer are automatically considered to be a disability for the purposes of the Equality Act, thereby requiring employers to make reasonable adjustments. However, in this context any adjustments, including flexible working where applicable, would only be required on a temporary basis, perhaps whilst treatment is ongoing or during recovery. In such circumstances, a permanent change to terms and conditions of employment would not be required.

It should be noted that, in addition to the legislation relating to flexible working applications discussed in Chapter 1, a separate legal framework also applies. Employees may still make a request in the same way under an organization's normal policy, but employers must also consider their obligations under the Equality Act in addition to making a decision purely based on the statutory grounds and process. A failure to do so could amount to disability discrimination. Advice, including medical advice where appropriate, should be taken on the specific circumstances of each case.

Carers

According to figures from Carers UK, 1 in 7 of the workforce is providing care for someone who is elderly, seriously ill or disabled. The majority of carers are women (approximately 58 per cent). 1 in 6 carers reduce their hours or leave the workforce altogether to enable them to provide this care. Around 600 people give up their job every day – a significant loss of talent and skills. There is also an increase in what is known as the 'sandwich carer' – someone who is providing care for their children whilst simultaneously caring for an older relative. People are most likely to be carers between the ages of 45 and 64. An ageing population means that this situation is only likely to increase in the years to come. Without flexible forms of working, this group may be excluded from the traditional 9 to 5 workforce.

Carers in the UK have few statutory employment rights and no formal right to time off from work, outside of the fairly limited rights to time off for dependants in an emergency situation. 1 in 3 carers report that they do not receive any support from their employer (Carers UK, 2019). There are many ways in which organizations can do so – and flexible working is just one such approach.

One of the elements of a flexible workplace discussed in the previous chapter identified flexibility in all its forms as a key element. The flexibility demanded by carers provides a further example of this in practice. Some carers may want or need a more traditional form of flexible working such as part-time hours due to the level of demand resulting from their caring responsibilities. However, caring needs can vary significantly and sometimes at short notice, which means that a formal, regular arrangement may not allow the employee to balance their sometimes competing responsibilities effectively. For example, carers may be required to accompany the person for whom they care for hospital appointments, the times and duration of which may vary or be out of their control. In the event of caring for someone with a serious illness, symptoms and needs may fluctuate very quickly. There may also be occasions when flexibility to provide care is only needed on a short-term basis, perhaps following medical treatment. In these circumstances there is little value in requiring an employee to complete the lengthy statutory process.

A supportive and flexible employer can be the critical difference between a carer being able to continue to work or not – and it is an example of where flexible working needs to get creative. Flexible working in this context needs to include the ability to flex the flexible, trialling and experimenting with working patterns that can adapt to changing circumstances. Without flexibility, these thousands of workers, many of whom will be at the peak of their skills, knowledge and experience, may find themselves excluded from the labour market, and businesses in turn lose out on potential talent. This provides further evidence to support the idea that employers need to change their overall mindset towards flexible working, not merely address it on a case-by-case basis.

Older workers

People are working longer and living longer than ever before – and as discussed in Chapter 3 this has implications for the future of work. For the last two centuries life expectancy has risen by around three years every decade. The UK state retirement age has increased, and in 2019 the government confirmed it was considering raising the retirement age to 75 by 2035. Currently more than 1 million workers in the UK are over 65, a figure that has been increasing for well over a decade. Following the introduction of age discrimination legislation, there is no longer a UK default retirement age. The nature of pensions has also changed significantly with fewer and fewer organizations offering lucrative, defined-benefit schemes and transferring the responsibility of retirement savings to individuals.

According to the Office for National Statistics, the number of employees in work after 65 is continuing to rise. There were 10.4 per cent (1.19 million) people aged 65 and over in employment in the period May to July 2016. In the same period for 2006, 6.6 per cent (609,000) of the 65+ population had a job. These figures can be separated into 742,000 men and 448,000 women. Taking a longer-term view, under existing legislation, the number of people of UK state pension age and over is projected to increase by 32.5 per cent from 12.4 million in mid-2015 to 16.5 million by mid-2039 (ONS, 2016). These figures together demonstrate that the older worker will be a significant source of talent for the future – and talent that may well wish to continue to work past what is currently viewed as the typical retirement age. Flexible working, therefore, can be an attractive alternative to full retirement – once again further illustrating that flexible working is not just for a small group of employees but has broad appeal.

There may be many reasons why someone wants to work past the current typical retirement age. Continuing to work may be a financial decision, or simply a lifestyle choice. Some older workers may wish to combine work with caring for younger members of their family, or they may wish to get involved in other leisure activities. However, whilst some employees do not want to retire, it does not follow that employees will necessarily want to work the way, or indeed the hours, that they have for most of their career, which for many people will have been the default, full-time working week. Flexible working can help organizations retain the valuable skills, knowledge and experience of older workers, whilst providing greater choice for individuals at the same time. Phased retirement is one form of flexibility, specifically targeted at older workers, during which employees typically reduce their working hours over an agreed period (sometimes months or years), ultimately taking full retirement. This is sometimes combined with a change of role, perhaps to one with less responsibility or seniority. This is, however, only one option, and still assumes that the ultimate goal of the individual is to leave the workforce entirely. All of the forms of flexible working discussed in Chapter 1 are potentially of interest to older workers seeking greater flexibility over the way that they work.

Menopause

There is another stage of life during which employees may welcome flexible working: the menopause. In recent years we have become increasingly aware of the menopause as a workplace issue and it is not uncommon now to find organizations taking a proactive stance in supporting women through this life stage, including launching menopause policies or training for people managers. Women comprise approximately half (47 per cent) of the UK's workforce. Of employed people aged over 50, 45 per cent are women, representing 3.5 million workers – in fact, women over 50 are the fastest-growing segment of the workforce (CIPD, 2019b). Thus, many of today's women workers are or will be working through the menopause and managing the associated symptoms at work. Symptoms of the menopause can vary widely, with some women experiencing significant symptoms and impacts upon their life. Studies show that some women felt the menopause had negatively affected their job performance, including a belief that it had a negative impact on their managers' and colleagues' perceptions of their competence at work (CIPD, 2019b). Managing symptoms in the workplace can also lead to increased levels of stress.

The variable symptoms associated with menopause can be supported through flexible working. Examples include allowing staff to work around their symptoms, perhaps by allowing them to rest when they are tired and make the time up later, or permitting occasional homeworking when symptoms are severe. Some women experiencing the menopause will find that they have times of the day when symptoms are more or less problematic and start and finish times could be adjusted to take this into account. For example, women with disturbed sleep patterns may find they are more productive with a later start time. Flexibility around break and rest times is another potential adjustment from which some employees may benefit. In 2019 the CIPD published guidance on supporting employees through the menopause that included examples and policies from forward-thinking employers, some of which highlight flexible working as a mechanism of support.

Key takeaways

- Flexible working can support improvements in workplace equality, diversity and inclusion – but only where necessary culture change takes place at the same time.
- Flexible working can support organizations in tackling their gender pay gap by increasing opportunities for quality part-time work as well as challenging stereotypes about who works flexibly.

- As well as supporting working parents, flexible working can help to open up the labour market to talent pools who may otherwise be excluded from (or not wish to undertake) the default working model, such as employees with disabilities, older workers and carers.

- Organizations can use the offer of flexible working as a way to target a diverse range of potential job candidates, also helping to enhance their employer brand and reputation as a fair and flexible employer.

- Flexible working can help to challenge society's traditional gender roles – but can also have the unintended consequence of reinforcing them too. Care needs to be taken in implementation to reduce this potential.

- Flexible working alone cannot tackle some of these big, structural and systemic issues – but it can be part of a range of solutions to support greater inclusion in the workplace.

References

Carers UK (2019) *Facts about carers*, www.carersuk.org/images/Facts_about_ Carers_2019.pdf (archived at https://perma.cc/ZS6M-J4CQ)

Chung, H (2018) Gender, flexibility stigma and the perceived negative consequences of flexible working in the UK, *Social Indicators Research*, doi. org/10.1007/s11205-018-2036-7 (archived at https://perma.cc/X2SU-VXBG)

Chung, H (2019a) 'Women's work penalty' in access to flexible working arrangements across Europe, *European Journal of Industrial Relations*, vol 25, Issue 1, doi.org/10.1177/0959680117752829 (archived at https://perma.cc/ ZV3U-XW79)

Chung, H (2019b) *Flexible Working Can Reinforce Gender Stereotypes*, The Conversation, theconversation.com/flexible-working-can-reinforce-gender-stereotypes-109158 (archived at https://perma.cc/GEV5-68W3)

Chung, H and van der Horst, M (2017) Women's employment patterns after childbirth and the perceived access to and use of flexi time and teleworking, *Human Relations*, vol 71, Issue 1, pp 47–72, journals.sagepub.com/doi/ full/10.1177/0018726717713828 (archived at https://perma.cc/2G3Q-EC39)

Chung, H and van der Lippe, T (2018) Flexible working, work-life balance and gender equality: Introduction, *Social Indicators Research*, doi.org/10.1007/ s11205-018-2025-x (archived at https://perma.cc/78H2-YT94)

CIPD (2019a) *Diversity and Inclusion in the Workplace*, www.cipd.co.uk/ knowledge/fundamentals/relations/diversity/factsheet#6424 (archived at https://perma.cc/73F5-VSLC)

CIPD (2019b) *The Menopause At Work: A practical guide for managers*, CIPD, Londo www.cipd.co.uk/Images/menopause-guide-for-people-managers_tcm18-55548.pdf (archived at https://perma.cc/Z744-5VE4)

Deloitte (2019) *The Millennial Dad at Work Report*, in association with Daddilife, www.daddilife.com/wp-content/uploads/2019/05/The-Millenial-Dad-at-Work-Report-2019.pdf (archived at https://perma.cc/K8MV-NSSH)

Fagan, C, Hegewisch, A and Pillinger, J (2006) *Out of Time – Why Britain needs a new approach to working time flexibility*, Trades Union Congress

Jones, L (2019) *Women's Progression in the Workplace*, Government Equalities Office, assets.publishing.service.gov.uk/government/uploads/system/uploads/attachment_data/file/840404/KCL_Main_Report.pdf (archived at https://perma.cc/8AJN-PTSS)

Leslie, L, Park, T and Mehng, S (2012) Flexible working practices: A source of career premiums or penalties? *Academy of Management Journal*, vol 55, No 6, pp 1407–428

Munsch, C (2016) Flexible work, flexible penalties: The effect of gender, childcare and type of request on flexibility bias, *Social Forces*, vol 94, pp 1567–591

Office for National Statistics (2016) *Five Facts About Older People At Work*, www.ons.gov.uk/employmentandlabourmarket/peopleinwork/employmentandemployeetypes/articles/fivefactsaboutolderpeopleatwork/2016-10-01 (archived at https://perma.cc/GN6L-VCQB)

Office for National Statistics (2018a) *Disability Pay Gaps in the UK 2018*, www.ons.gov.uk/peoplepopulationandcommunity/healthandsocialcare/disability/articles/disabilitypaygapsintheuk/2018 (archived at https://perma.cc/HX4X-BUKN)

Office for National Statistics (2018b) *The Commuting Gap: Men account for 65% of commutes lasting more than an hour*, www.ons.gov.uk/employmentandlabourmarket/peopleinwork/employmentandemployeetypes/articles/thecommutinggapmenaccountfor65ofcommuteslastingmorethananhour/2018-11-07 (archived at https://perma.cc/S4MG-V7BW)

Office for National Statistics (2019) *Gender Pay Gap in the UK 2019*, www.ons.gov.uk/employmentandlabourmarket/peopleinwork/earningsandworkinghours/bulletins/genderpaygapintheuk/2019 (archived at https://perma.cc/57U2-QAT3)

Women and Equalities Committee (2016) *Gender Pay Gap: Second report of session 2015-16*, House of Commons, publications.parliament.uk/pa/cm201516/cmselect/cmwomeq/584/584.pdf (archived at https://perma.cc/6TAU-X4KQ)

Working Families (2011) *Working and Fathers: Combining family life and work*, www.workingfamilies.org.uk/wp-content/uploads/2014/09/WF_WorkingAndFathers-Report-FINAL.pdf (archived at https://perma.cc/ZHY6-NLYA)

Workingmums (2019) *A fifth of parents leaving jobs due to childcare costs*, www.workingmums.co.uk/a-fifth-of-parents-leaving-jobs-due-to-childcare-costs/ (archived at https://perma.cc/5LRY-QMWC)

05

Flexible working and wellbeing

Employee wellbeing continues to increase in importance for many organizations. This is not surprising, particularly when we consider the high incidence of mental-health-related absence from work – for most organizations today, mental ill-health is the primary cause of employee absence. Stress is rising year on year and long working hours are increasingly the norm in many organizations today (Cooper and Hesketh, 2019).

The UK in particular has a work–life balance problem. According to international standards, the work–life balance of UK workers ranks 25th out of 25 comparator economies (CIPD, 2019). Working hours are long and many employees report working longer than their contracted, paid hours. The same CIPD research found that 24 per cent of employees said they found it difficult to relax in their personal time as a result of their job. Add to this the potential for technology to spill work activities into our home lives and we have real potential for a toxic combination resulting in poor workplace wellbeing – something no reasonable employer should ignore.

This chapter will explore flexible working in the context of wellbeing. Drawing on research it will seek to understand how flexible working can enhance wellbeing, as well as consider the potential wellbeing issues that might be caused by working flexibly. Flexible working has the potential to support improved employee wellbeing in a number of ways, by lessening the impact of commuting either by reducing it (in respect of homeworking) or enabling employees to commute outside of core hours. It can also reduce the cost of commuting, noting that financial pressures can also be a source of stress and anxiety in their own right. Flexible working can support employees to balance their work and broader life more effectively, including enabling them to undertake both work and caring responsibilities. The evidence will, however, show that flexible working is not a wellbeing panacea and care must be taken on implementation if benefits are to be realized and any negative consequences avoided.

What is wellbeing?

What exactly do we mean when we talk about wellbeing? It is a term that has many definitions. Historically, two ideas about wellbeing have emerged; these are known as the eudemonic and hedonic approaches. The *eudemonic* approach looks at overall life satisfaction, having a purpose to life and the ability of each individual to reach their full potential. In contrast, the *hedonic* approach focuses on subjective wellbeing, happiness and pleasure (Cooper and Hesketh, 2019). Another definition of wellbeing is proposed by the World Health Organization, who defines it as 'where each individual realizes their own potential, can cope with the normal stresses of life, can work productively and fruitfully, and is able to make a contribution to their community'.

Wellbeing is a term that is used by academics but is also in everyday use, often associated with many different ideas around happiness, thriving, flourishing and life satisfaction. The New Economics Foundation describes wellbeing as simply 'feeling good and functioning well' (NEF, 2008).

Turning to wellbeing in the workplace, the CIPD refers to a 'healthy workplace that helps people to flourish and reach their potential'.

Wellbeing is therefore something of an ill-defined term, and will undoubtedly mean different things to different people, both at home and at work. This presents a particular challenge when seeking to understand the implications of flexible working on employee wellbeing.

Benefits of workplace wellbeing

The CIPD published a *Health and Wellbeing at Work 2019* survey that identified three main benefits of employers increasing their focus on employee wellbeing:

- better employee morale and engagement;
- a healthier and more inclusive culture;
- lower sickness absence.

Organizations that invest in wellbeing programmes report a range of benefits from doing so, including the above three as well as reduced levels of work-related stress, enhanced employer brand, improved retention and improved productivity (CIPD, 2019). It is therefore not surprising to find that many organizations are now increasing their focus on employee wellbeing – and flexible working is just one of many supporting actions that organizations can take as part of a wellbeing strategy.

There are many factors that can influence employee wellbeing, either positively or negatively. These can be divided into situational factors (those relating to the job or organization), or factors that relate to the individual themselves (such as their overall health or personal attitude). Situational factors include the content of the job itself, workload, working hours, work–life balance, control, available support and resources and the organizational culture (Arnold and Randall, 2010).

There are three broad types of wellbeing intervention typically undertaken by organizations:

- Primary interventions which aim to tackle organization-wide issues including culture and organizational design. These seek to prevent work-related ill-health from arising.

- Secondary interventions that operate at the individual level, helping employees to cope with work-related stressors. These could include resilience training, stress workshops, mindfulness or exercise classes.

- Tertiary interventions such as occupational health, employee assistance programmes or counselling that help to support employees who are already suffering from ill-health (work-related or otherwise).

Research suggests that primary interventions are more effective than secondary, and secondary are more effective than tertiary – the optimum position for any wellbeing strategy is to have all three interventions taking place at the same time (Arnold and Randall, 2010). However, many organizational wellbeing programmes, opportunities and interventions operate primarily in the secondary and tertiary space, quite possibly because these are easier and quicker to introduce. This has led to criticism of wellbeing initiatives as being too focused on the symptoms of ill-health at work, rather than tackling its broader (sometimes structural or systemic) causes. Despite these criticisms, wellbeing at work remains an important consideration for many organizations in terms of its impact on productivity, costs, engagement and morale.

Stress and mental health

Stress and mental health is a significant cause of absence from work, and as such of particular interest to organizations. In the UK, it is the primary reason why employees take sickness absence. In 2018/19, 12.8 million working days were lost to work-related stress, depression and anxiety– this is 44 per cent of all working days lost due to ill-health (HSE, 2019). These are significant numbers, although it is likely that in reality the number is even higher than reported as some employees, concerned about stigma, will misreport the reasons for mental-health-related absence. According to re-search by the charity Mind, around a third of employees disagreed with the statement 'I would feel able to talk openly with my line manager if I was feeling stressed' (Mind, 2019).

With these statistics, it is clear why supporting positive mental health and addressing work-related stress is a primary focus of many employee well-being strategies and interventions.

The UK Health and Safety Executive has published standards that cover the primary causes of stress in the workplace. These are:

- work demands – workloads and work patterns;
- control – how much say someone has over the way that they work;
- support – from line managers and colleagues;
- relationships – including dealing with inappropriate behaviour and addressing conflict;
- role – whether people understand their role and the nature of the work itself;
- change – how organizational change is managed and communicated.

As we can see, one factor that is known to cause stress is the extent to which the employee has control over the way that they undertake their work. Low levels of control can add to stress levels, and high levels of control can help to reduce it. Flexible working can enable employees to have greater control over when and where they work than do those employees who have more structured working arrangements. Research supports this position; flexible working arrangements can benefit employees through the reduction of work-related stress through reducing work–life conflict, commuting stress and interruptions (Clarke and Holdsworth, 2017). However, other causes of stress detailed by the HSE could, without careful management, be increased by flexible working; for example, where managers are not supportive or where workload is not adjusted to take into account changes to workload when working hours are reduced. This is an argument for ensuring that the introduction of flexible working arrangements is supported by effective line manager training and support mechanisms.

The highly individual and subjective nature of wellbeing, combined with the many forms of flexible working leads to varying outcomes when it comes to stress and mental health. Research by the University of Cranfield found that some employees who work reduced hours report lower levels of stress than those who do not work flexibly. Some respondents to the survey said that having time away from work acted as a pressure valve for them, therefore benefiting their mental health. Conversely, other respondents said that for them, working a reduced-hours schedule was actually a cause of stress, as they found themselves under pressure to complete their work in a shorter time frame (Kelliher and Anderson, 2010).

As with all wellbeing interventions, its subjective and personal nature means that there is no one best way to enable employee wellbeing. What will help one person improve their wellbeing will not necessarily work for another. For some employees, flexible working may have a positive impact on their overall levels of stress. For others, it may have no impact at all, or be the cause of additional stress. In the introduction to this book we considered the extent to which flexible working was a shift towards an adult-to-adult relationship in the workplace, whereby people could be empowered to work in the way that suits them best. This applies to flexible working and wellbeing too; empowerment means that the employee chooses the working pattern that causes them the least amount of stress, whatever that looks like.

Commuting

For some employees, commuting to and from work can be a source of stress and anxiety in itself. Two out of five workers define commuting as the worst part of their day (International Working Group, 2019). Commutes are getting longer too. The 2018 ONS data showed that the number of people commuting for more than an hour to get to work has risen by 31 per cent since 2011. A 2019 YouGov/Lloyds Bank UK-wide survey found that employees on average spend more than 10 days a year (251 hours) commuting, with 1 in 5 commuters saying that their commute has become less reliable in the last five years and a third saying it is more crowded. These figures will perhaps be no surprise to many regular commuters.

Research from the Office for National Statistics (conducted in 2014) considered the impact of commuting on four measures of wellbeing: overall life satisfaction; the sense that one's life was worthwhile; and levels of happiness and anxiety the previous day. The results were statistically significant for each of the four aspects of personal wellbeing measured: after holding other factors constant, life satisfaction, the sense that one's activities are worthwhile, and happiness all decreased with each successive minute of travel. Meanwhile, average anxiety levels increased with each additional minute of the commute. Average happiness levels begin to fall and anxiety begins to rise after the first 15 minutes of travel time, suggesting again that daily emotions are particularly affected by commuting. The worst effects of commuting on personal wellbeing were associated with journey times lasting between 61 and 90 minutes.

This research also considered the impact on wellbeing of modes of travel. They found that people who take the train to work (around 5 per cent of the population) had higher anxiety levels on average than those who travelled in a private vehicle. The survey also found that those who travel by bus had a lower sense of overall life satisfaction and a feeling that their day-to-day activities were worthwhile.

The findings demonstrated that commuting has a negative impact on personal wellbeing and that (perhaps unsurprisingly) in general longer commutes are worse for personal wellbeing than shorter commutes. These negative impacts were not found to be offset by higher incomes (Office for National Statistics, 2014). It seems therefore that money cannot buy wellbeing.

Using public transport can reduce the control that employees have over their travel arrangements – and as we have already seen from the HSE, a lack of control is a particular source of work-related stress. Many forms of public transport are unreliable and overcrowded. Recent years have seen many high-profile issues particularly with the train networks in the UK, coupled with rising costs. There is, therefore, strong evidence that many forms of commuting are not good for our personal levels of wellbeing.

Homeworking or remote working (either full-time or for just part of the working week) can be a potential alternative to commuting some or all of the time. Other forms of flexible working such as flexi-time or staggered hours can also help employees to reduce the stressors caused by commuting during peak times. Finally, the overall reduction of commuting time can provide employees with more time with which to balance their work and other commitments. Reducing commuting (through homeworking) may also mean that employees do not arrive at work exhausted by their commute, and are able to be more effective and have more energy for the day ahead.

However, not all of the research suggests an entirely positive picture. Care must also be taken to support staff who work remotely. A 2017 Eurofound/ILO report found that 41 per cent of remote workers reported high stress levels, compared to just 25 per cent of office workers. Some remote or homeworkers also report feeling isolated, lonely, unable to switch off and lacking in social relationships (Russell, 2019). These factors may vary depending on the number of days that someone works remotely. Whilst these findings do not on their own mean that wellbeing will be negatively impacted by home- or remote working, it does further highlight the need for effective policies, procedures and approaches to flexible working arrangements; organizations cannot simply assume that everyone will be able to adapt to new ways of working without support.

Work–life balance

Work–life balance is another concept that is difficult to define and means different things to different people. It is generally taken to mean the balance found by an individual between their work responsibilities and non-work aspects of their life such as family, home and hobbies. However it may be defined, we know that many employees find it hard to get the balance that they want or need.

The UK has a culture of long hours working that can be a cause of difficulty for employees, particularly in relation to balancing their work and other priorities and commitments. It can also lead to work–life conflict. For example, around a third of employees report that their job prevents them from spending enough time with their partner or family (Fagan *et al*, 2011). Long hours working is also associated with high levels of stress (Chandola *et al*, 2019). This all too typical feature of many workplaces has a negative impact on families, personal lives and individual health and wellbeing (Fagan *et al*, 2006). Flexible working may seem like part of the answer to this issue, but research suggests that remote workers can often end up working longer hours than their office-based colleagues (Cooper and Hesketh, 2019). Conversely, some forms of flexible working that involve reduced-hours working may be beneficial in reducing chronic stress in employees when compared to their full-time colleagues (Chandola *et al*, 2019). Again we can see from these two viewpoints the complexity of understanding the implications of flexible working and general wellbeing.

Poor work–life balance can have a negative impact on individual job-related performance and thus the organization itself (Fagan *et al*, 2011). There is research that indicates flexible working arrangements can help employees to enhance their work–life balance as well as reduce work–family conflict. One such survey from the CIPD found that 65 per cent of flexible workers were satisfied or very satisfied with their work–life balance compared with 47 per cent of employees who do not work flexibly (CIPD, 2016). This is a significant difference. Broadly, the evidence across four major meta-analyses of the association between flexible working arrangements and work–life conflict found that greater flexibility is associated with lower levels of conflict (Allen *et al*, 2013).

Like other aspects of wellbeing, work–life balance is subjective in nature; what feels like an acceptable balance for one individual will not necessarily work for someone else with different life circumstances or commitments. Work–life balance is not simply the personal challenge of the employee, but something over which employers can have significant influence, as well as provide a range of support.

Wellbeing conclusions

Despite the broadly positive nature of research into the links between flexible working and wellbeing and work–life balance, the overall picture is complicated, as different forms of flexible working, as well as who is using them and why, can lead to very different wellbeing outcomes for individuals. For example, women may find that some forms of flexible working (such as homeworking) will lead to an expansion of work or increase the domestic burden upon them – or indeed both. There is also the risk of what has been termed the 'gift exchange'; the idea that employees feel they have been gifted flexibility by their employers and must therefore work harder or longer than they otherwise would have in return for that perceived benefit (Chung and van der Lippe, 2018).

There are other challenges to be mindful of, particularly in relation to homeworking. Working from home can support employees to achieve a better work–life balance through making it easier to make care arrangements or reduce commuting times. However, a 2017 ILO report found that 41 per cent of remote workers reported high stress levels, compared to just 25 per cent of office workers (Eurofound/ILO, 2017). Another *Harvard Business Review* study highlighted how regular homeworkers often feel left out and can experience negative impacts on their work relationships as a result of not being physically in the same location as colleagues (*Harvard Business Review*, 2017). Furthermore, homeworking can lead to the blurring of boundaries between work and home which can be a stressor in its own right, an 'overspill' of work into the home sphere making it difficult to switch off – a potential challenge to wellbeing and work–life balance. Combined with the potential for feelings of isolation and fewer opportunities for important social relationships, it is clear that care must be taken to ensure that flexible working does not have negative wellbeing implications. This will be a joint responsibility between employee, manager and the organization via its overall approach to flexible working.

When introducing flexibility, care must also be taken to avoid the potential of work intensification – the increase of workload and working time, a subject discussed initially in Chapter 2. When working flexibly, employees may find that work can intensify in a number of ways. Firstly, there are some forms of flexible working that make it easier to work harder or longer. For example, when employees work from home they may have fewer distractions or take fewer breaks than they would in a traditional environment such as an office. Some people report starting or finishing work at the same time that they would if they were commuting to their workplaces, thereby adding to the length of their working day, or working at times that they are not scheduled to work, such as taking phone calls or responding to emails on non-working days or times. Part-time workers (or those with time flexibility) may find that they are less fatigued or are working at times that better suit them, rather than the default model, meaning that they may sometimes work more or harder. Employees may also feel that they have to work harder as an act of reciprocation, and will thus make a range of sacrifices or increase their efforts. Finally, flexible workers may feel that they have to work harder to meet the expectations of managers and colleagues, fearing negative perceptions of their flexibility (Kelliher and Anderson, 2010). This research found that work intensification was a very real problem for both reduced-hours and remote workers. Interestingly, however, those employees reporting work intensification also reported more positive scores on measures for job satisfaction and organization commitment than those who do not work flexibly, further underlying the point that when it comes to wellbeing and flexible working, the overall picture is far from straightforward.

Effective communication, manager training and wellness initiatives designed with homeworkers in mind can work together to ensure that employees can achieve the wellbeing benefits of flexibility, whilst minimizing any downsides. Organizations should look to include work–life balance support to flexible workers as part of their overall approach to flexible working implementation. Put simply, some employees will need help to understand that whilst flexible working means that they can work from anywhere and any when, this does not mean that they *have* to do so.

It is important to remember that flexible working can form part of a range of wellbeing interventions provided by the organization for the benefit of its employees. Given its highly personal and subjective nature, there is no one wellbeing solution that will work for all employees. Good wellbeing programmes will provide employees with choice and autonomy to enable their own wellbeing in a way that meets their own particular needs; in many ways this is the essence of flexible working – increased employee choice and control.

Flexible working is not a silver bullet for employee wellbeing; the subjective and individual nature of wellbeing, combined with the many different forms of flexible working mean that flexible working on its own will not address structural and systemic issues that negatively impact employee wellbeing. The extent to whether flexible working in its own right can deliver individual wellbeing improvements varies according to the particular type of flexible working undertaken. As with other wellbeing initiatives, some people will benefit from flexible working, whereas others may not. Of course, it is not just employees who benefit from improved work–life balance; there are benefits too for employers in terms of a healthier and happier workforce, improved productivity and reduced absenteeism (Fagan *et al*, 2011).

Where flexible working within an organization becomes a norm rather than an exception, it is much easier for employees to use flexible arrangements to improve their work–life balance (Chung and van der Lippe, 2018). Perhaps then as flexible working diffuses through society and organizations, some of the potential negative consequences discussed here will reduce. Only time will tell if this will be the case.

KEY TAKEAWAYS

- Workplace wellbeing is an area of increasing interest to organizations, and many organizations are implementing wellbeing programmes and initiatives to support their employees.

- Flexible working can help to tackle a range of wellbeing-related issues, from commuting stress to balancing work and caring responsibilities, and can form part of a broader wellbeing programme.

- Flexible working can support wellbeing and work–life balance, but the extent to which this can be achieved depends on a variety of factors including the worker's own personal situation and the type of flexible working undertaken.

- Flexible working, especially where the worker has high autonomy over their schedule, can help employees to reduce stressors, especially those caused by commuting, and find an effective work–life balance.

- Flexible working can also impact negatively on wellbeing if it is not managed well; for example, homeworkers may find that the boundaries between work and home are blurred or part-time workers may experience work intensification – care must be taken by organizations to prevent these negative impacts arising, and managers can be particularly important in ensuring this does not occur.

- Employers should not assume that flexible working will automatically be good for employee wellbeing – the subjective and individual nature of wellbeing means that what will enhance wellbeing for some will not necessarily support another.

References

Allen, T, Johnson, R, Kiburz, K and Shockley, K (2013) Work–family conflict and flexible work arrangements: deconstructing flexibility, *Personnel Psychology*, vol 66, Issue 2, onlinelibrary.wiley.com/doi/abs/10.1111/peps.12012 (archived at https://perma.cc/R2VZ-GWYY)

Arnold, J and Randall, R (2010) *Work Psychology: Understanding human behaviour in the workplace*, 5th edn, Financial Times/ Prentice Hall

Chandola, T, Booker, C, Kumari, M and Benzeval, M (2019) Are flexible working arrangements associated with lower levels of stress related biomarkers? A study of 6,025 employers in the UK, Longitudinal Study, *Sociology*, vol 53, Issue 4, pp 779–99

Chung, H and van der Lippe, T (2018) Flexible working: work life balance and gender equality, *Social Indicators Research*, doi.org/10.1007/s11205-018-2025-x (archived at https://perma.cc/78H2-YT94)

CIPD (2016) *Employee Outlook, Employee Views on Working Life: Focus on commuting and flexible working*, CIPD, London

CIPD (2019) *Health and Wellbeing at Work Report 2019*, CIPD, www.cipd.co.uk/Images/health-and-well-being-at-work-2019.v1_tcm18-55881.pdf (archived at https://perma.cc/4NRU-GZGX)

Clarke, S and Holdsworth, L (2017) *Flexibility in the Workplace: Implications of flexible working arrangements for individuals, teams and organizations*, Acas, archive.acas.org.uk/media/4901/Flexibility-in-the-Workplace-Implications-of-flexible-work-arrangements-for-individuals-teams-and-organizations/pdf/Flexibility-in-the-Workplace.pdf (archived at https://perma.cc/52XB-KTJ7)

Cooper, C and Hesketh, I (2019) *Wellbeing at Work: How to design, implement and evaluate an effective strategy*, Kogan Page, London

Eurofound/International Labour Office (2017) *Working Anytime, Anywhere: The effects on the world of work*, Publications Office of the European Union, Luxembourg, and the International Labour Office, Geneva, www.eurofound.europa.eu/publications/report/2017/working-anytime-anywhere-the-effects-on-the-world-of-work (archived at https://perma.cc/8W7W-3DQ5)

Fagan, C, Hegewisch, A and Pillinger, J (2006) *Out of Time: Why Britain needs a new approach to working-time flexibility*, Trades Union Congress, www.researchgate.net/publication/286447808_Out_of_Time_-_why_Britain_needs_a_new_approach_to_working-time_flexibility (archived at https://perma.cc/B87P-XQRV)

Fagan, C, Lyonette, C, Smith, M and Saldana-Tejeda, A (2011) *The Influence of Working Time Arrangements on Work-Life Integration or 'Balance': A review of the international evidence*, Conditions of Work and Employment Series No.32, International Labour Office, www.ilo.org/wcmsp5/groups/public/---ed_protect/---protrav/---travail/documents/publication/wcms_187306.pdf (archived at https://perma.cc/R4DK-8ANK)

Harvard Business Review (2017) A study of 1,100 employees found that remote workers feel shunned and left out, *Harvard Business Review*, hbr.org/2017/11/a-study-of-1100-employees-found-that-remote-workers-feel-shunned-and-left-out (archived at https://perma.cc/VJ3H-5Q85)

HSE (2019) *Work-Related Stress, Anxiety or Depression Statistics in Great Britain 2019*, Health and Safety Executive, www.hse.gov.uk/statistics/causdis/stress.pdf (archived at https://perma.cc/2AFV-Y5EJ)

HSE (nd) What are the management standards?, www.hse.gov.uk/stress/standards/ (archived at https://perma.cc/9LQQ-YR5W)

International Working Group (2019) *Welcome to Generation Flex: The employee power shift*, assets.regus.com/pdfs/iwg-workplace-survey/iwg-workplace-survey-2019.pdf (archived at https://perma.cc/PR9P-84RE)

Kelliher, C and Anderson, D (2010) Doing more with less? Flexible working practices and the intensification of work, *Human Relations*, vol 63, doi: 10.1177/0018726709349199

Mind (2019) Taking care of your staff, www.mind.org.uk/workplace/mental-health-at-work/taking-care-of-your-staff/ (archived at https://perma.cc/94VG-P7XC)

New Economics Foundation (2008) *Five Ways to Wellbeing*, neweconomics.org/uploads/files/8984c5089d5c2285ee_t4m6bhqq5.pdf (archived at https://perma.cc/44DE-5H7Z)

Office for National Statistics (2014) *Commuting and Personal Wellbeing Survey*, webarchive.nationalarchives.gov.uk/20160131203938/ (archived at https://perma.cc/W3VW-N3ZV) http://www.ons.gov.uk/ons/rel/wellbeing/measuring-national-well-being/commuting-and-personal-well-being--2014/art-commuting-and-personal-well-being.html#tab-2--Key-Points (archived at https://perma.cc/HH9H-NBAN)

Russell, S (2019) *How Remote Working Can Increase Stress and Reduce Well-Being*, The Conversation, theconversation.com/how-remote-working-can-increase-stress-and-reduce-well-being-125021?utm_medium=email&utm_campaign=Latest%20from%20The%20Conversation%20for%20October%2014%202019%20-%201433913578&utm_content=Latest%20from%20The%20Conversation%20for%20October%2014%202019%20-%201433913578+CID_6f83680f2a20c2e64e7e6ffe1e5702ef&utm_source=campaign_monitor_uk&utm_term=increase%20stress (archived at https://perma.cc/7GC4-9BGS)

YouGov/Lloyds Bank (2019) www.yourmoney.com/household-bills/british-workers-spend-492-days-of-their-lives-travelling-to-work/ (archived at https://perma.cc/ZW7E-4S5B)

06

Exploring flexible working myths

Despite the many evidenced benefits of flexible working, there are also a significant number of myths (mostly with negative connotations) associated with it. Some of these myths have already been briefly discussed; this chapter will explore them in more detail. Myths may operate as barriers in their own right, both to individuals seeking flexibility as well as to broader organizational adoption and culture change.

These myths range from assumptions about who would want to work flexibly to the practical aspects of dealing with requests and even the attitudes of flexible workers. Some of these myths are interconnected; when present in an organization, all of them can have very real implications for the availability and success of flexible working, as well as having significant career implications for some employees. Whilst some myths are practical in nature and easily challenged with simple explanations or data (such as those relating to misconceptions about policy and process), others are much more deeply embedded and linked to wider organizational culture issues and personal bias. Consequently, these myths are harder to shatter.

In this chapter we will consider and challenge some of the most common misconceptions about flexible working as well as the evidence that can rebut them, but let us first begin by considering two important and fundamental myths that go to the very heart of flexible working: the default model of work and the idea of the 'ideal worker'. These two myths often work hand in hand; they are at the heart of why, despite evidence of the benefits of flexible working, it is not yet widely accepted in all organizations, and where it is, there can remain consequences for the individuals who opt to undertake it.

The ideal worker

The ideal worker prioritizes work over everything else. The ideal worker is available 24/7, committed to the organization and has high levels of motivation and engagement. The ideal worker will give discretionary effort and has few commitments outside of their work. The ideal worker will not take lots of sick leave, is always present and gets the job done, above and beyond expectations. The ideal worker will stay the course and get their long-service awards. The ideal worker also probably does not want to work flexibly, unless we count those forms of flexibility that benefit the organization such as remote working whilst on holiday or at the weekend. Where they do undertake this 'good' type of flexibility, it is likely to be rewarded in a way that flexible working to care for a family is not (Chung and van der Lippe, 2018). Men are much more likely to be ideal workers (Chung, 2018).

Flexible working policies deviate from this norm by introducing the idea that employees have other potentially competing priorities and that it is possible to desire something else: a good work–life balance. People who seek to use flexible working policies are therefore 'other': deviating from the ideal worker. Quite possibly, they are therefore less desirable as an employee – or at best tolerated. Those who do not fit the model face career marginalization (Wheatley, 2012) and other forms of flexibility stigma. It is the ideal worker myth that also encourages presenteeism and over-work and the glorification of business.

The ideal worker is a myth: he or she does not really exist. Every single employee, wherever they work and whatever their profession, will have priorities, desires and needs that are outside of or unrelated to their work. Few people are content to devote their entire lives to their work to the exclusion of everything else. Despite the reality, we still seek this ideal in the workplace and judge those who cannot meet it. We recruit in this image and too often merely tolerate alternatives. Herein lies the source of the stigma faced by flexible workers. The ideal worker is also a trap; whilst we continue to believe in it (or him or her), we will close our minds to other, talented individuals and whole new ways of working.

The 9 to 5 default model

This working pattern, referred to throughout this book as the default model, is a workplace tradition. We can trace the model back to the Industrial

Revolution, when work first moved out of our homes and our villages and into factories and then to offices.

A five-day working week with two days off for rest is typical for much of the world. Often the idea of a day (or days) of rest is linked to religious observance. Although there are variations between cultures and countries, a working week for many countries is approximately 40 hours, or an eight-hour working day. The eight-hour day also has its origins far back in history. After the Industrial Revolution, working very long hours was the norm; many people worked 12 hours a day or even longer. The campaign for an eight-hour day was led by a Welsh textile mill owner, Robert Owen. In 1817 he argued for 'eight hours' work, eight hours' recreation and eight hours' rest' for workers (TUC, 2019). It took many decades, however, before this became the accepted norm across the industrialized world, with many nations setting down limits on working hours in domestic legislation.

Up until the early 1900s, a six-day working week was commonplace, especially in manufacturing industries. Henry Ford was the instigator of change here; when Ford became one of the first employers to adopt a five-day working week in 1926 many other organizations followed suit. The outcome of this change for Ford and his contemporaries was increased productivity; output did not go down with reduced hours but instead increased. Nearly 100 years after Ford, in 2019, a campaign to move to a four-day working week began, making many of the same arguments about the potential gains of reducing the default working week even further; only time will tell if the idea will gain traction.

This is the history of our working pattern today. It was not deliberately designed but merely evolved according to the prevailing circumstances. So very much has changed since 1926, and yet so little has too. It is a myth that work needs to be organized in the default model; it is possible to work differently, should we choose to do so.

Together, the myths of the default model and the ideal worker combine to present a very real challenge to the acceptance and efficacy of flexible working. In their time, the ideas of Owen and Ford were revolutionary; they challenged the status quo – just like flexible working aims to do today. Before we can truly revolutionize work and working patterns, there are other myths that we must first shatter.

Other myths

Flexible working is not for our organization

This myth is an especially dangerous one. This is not just about flexible working; it is about change in general. We are cognitively biased towards the status quo, and usually the future is a mirror in which we can only see ourselves. When something new comes along that challenges our view of the world, some people will embrace it and others will hunker down and ignore it. The 'it does not apply here' myth has been uttered about many things (social media for business being a fairly recent example) and flexible working is merely the latest new thing for some to reject in this way. There are few organizations for which flexibility is entirely irrelevant; there are no organizations at all that can ignore the future of work.

Flexible workers are not committed

There is often a perception that when someone works flexibly (particularly part-time) they are somehow less committed to either their organization or their career – or indeed both. This is part of the wider issue around stigma that is associated with flexible working and impacts upon the career progression of flexible workers, a subject to which we will return later. This is another myth that can be rebutted with a range of evidence. In fact, academic research points to a range of studies that show part-time workers can in fact bring increased enthusiasm and energy to their workplace (Kelliher and Anderson, 2010).

Setting a precedent

There is often a prevailing myth that if a manager agrees to a single flexible working request from one member of staff this will somehow bind them to agreeing to all subsequent requests – or indeed that a single 'yes' will stimulate an unmanageable number of requests from employees; there will be an opening of the flexible floodgates.

It is true that when an Employment Tribunal considers how reasonable an employer has been in the event of a legal claim, consistency of approach can be a relevant factor. However, agreeing to a single flexible working request does not set a binding internal precedent. Managers may consider requests in the order in which they are received and on the basis of the current circumstances at the time of the request. Therefore, it is entirely feasible to say yes to one individual (for example, a request to work reduced hours) but say no to another similar request if it cannot then be accommodated. Such circumstances should, however, be very carefully managed and, where requests cannot be agreed, employees should be provided with a clear explanation to avoid grievances or reduced morale.

It is possible that when some employees begin to work flexibly this may lead to increased awareness of flexible working opportunities and this in turn may lead to additional requests being received. This does not have to be seen as a problem but rather a potential opportunity. If there are additional requests made, each request should be dealt with on its own merits. Instead of being concerned about an influx of requests, a helpful reframing of this situation is that additional requests are simply new opportunities to engage and motivate existing employees.

If I cannot see people working, they might take advantage

This is another myth which can be either openly expressed by managers or just implied in their actions or behaviours. It is not uncommon to find managers concerned that employees who are not being directly supervised, such as homeworkers or those working at different times to other team members, will skive or malinger. This perception is related to our traditional model of work where we all work in the same place and are generally visible to one another. Readers who have studied management or HR qualifications may well recall the traditional theories of motivation in the workplace. One well-known theory is Douglas McGregor's Theory X and Theory Y (Mullins, 2016). Theory Y assumes that workers can be trusted, are self-motivated, seek responsibility and can work on their own initiative. In contrast, Theory X stems from a position of low trust. Workers are assumed to be lazy and require constant supervision and direction, without which they will operate in their own self-interest. This leads to what is often known as 'command and control' type management. This theory might be several decades old, but many current workplace practices are still based on this world view. Although McGregor's theories represent a binary view of people management and motivation, the attitude that employees cannot be trusted if they cannot be seen derives firmly from a Theory X place, often deep-rooted in the culture of an organization. It is of course entirely possible that some employees, unsupervised, may fail to complete their tasks, take advantage or skive: this is, however, equally possible to achieve in a traditional workplace.

There are few workplaces in which an individual can be continuously monitored for performance, and in relation to knowledge work this is almost entirely impossible. Managers with this particular concern will require reassurance that there are processes through which this issue, if it arises, can be addressed.

Working with others needs to be face to face

Within many organizations the default position is that when there is a need for discussion or collaboration, a meeting takes place. Although technology provides us with viable alternatives, many meetings are face to face, regardless of the cost to the organization or the convenience of the attendees. In practice, the suggestion of online or virtual meetings is not well received. Where flexible working is in its infancy within a particular organization, a virtual meeting often means a single person on the end of the phone, struggling to follow the action of a room of people who have made no accommodation for their attendance. In his book *The Year Without Pants* Scott Berkun (2013) reflects on the fact that many people doubt that online meetings can work effectively, whilst overlooking the fact that many in-person meetings are also ineffective and unpopular.

We work face to face, we undertake meetings, because they are what we have always done. They are a workplace tradition. Challenging this myth can simply require demonstration of the alternatives – along with some support on using the relevant technology.

Managers cannot work flexibly

Another limiting belief that impacts upon the availability of flexible working arrangements is that flexible working is suitable only at, or suitable for, a certain level within an organization, and is not suitable for managerial or indeed senior roles. This particular myth can lead to employees 'stepping down' to positions of less responsibility in order to be able to work flexibly and making potentially unnecessary career compromises. These particular choices have a disproportionate impact on women who have had children. Leadership and management positions can be worked flexibly and there are many successful examples that show this myth up for the fiction that it is. Annually, flexible working company Timewise creates and publishes on its website its Power 50 awards, highlighting senior leaders who work flexibly, many of whom are working reduced hours or participating in job-shares, proof should it be required that people in senior positions can absolutely undertake flexible working where the organization is supportive. Where managers and senior leaders do work flexibly, it can provide a powerful role model for other employees and help to tackle this particular myth – and others. Sharing the success stories of senior flexible workers, the patterns that they work and how they make them effective can help to both drive culture change and provide 'permission' for others to seek the same.

Flexible workers are hard to manage

As a general objection to flexible working some managers will raise the concern that if individuals are working at a different time or in a different location to them or to the remainder of a team who undertake more traditional working patterns, this will somehow be more onerous than managing in the Monday to Friday, 9 to 5 tradition. Managing a flexible worker relies on trust, and on managing for results and outcomes rather than managing via presence. For some managers, this requires a mindset shift that will challenge their fundamental ideas about how management is undertaken. There is no evidence to suggest that flexible workers are more difficult to manage than their office-based, traditional-hours working contemporaries. Managers, however, may need to rethink *how* they manage. Regular one-to-one meetings, objective setting, performance reviews and regular communication are good practice for all managers in relation to managing their direct reports. Each of these becomes even more relevant in managing flexible workers. Managers can no longer rely necessarily on the 'water-cooler' meeting or incidental conversations. Interactions may need to be more deliberate, planned and focused. This does not necessarily mean doing anything above and beyond what is typically considered good management practice.

Flexible working means working fewer hours

Many people default to thinking that working flexibly means working less. As we have already seen in Chapter 1, there is much more to working flexibly than being part-time. Many forms of flexible working including annualized hours, compressed hours and nine-day fortnights still require employees to work the same number of hours as those undertaking a typical full-time week; they are simply organized differently to the traditional norm.

Flexible working is unsuitable for many roles

There are undoubtedly some role types and professions for which there are fewer opportunities for flexible working – or at least some forms of it. For example, a retail worker delivering face-to-face customer service will not have the ability to work from home and may not be able to have flexi-time. This should not, however, lead to assumptions about entire industries, organizations or specific job roles. A retail worker may be able to work other forms of flexibility such as self-rostering, job-sharing or compressed hours.

As with all new technologies or trends, it is easy for managers (or indeed whole organizations) to form a belief that these new approaches do not apply to them. There are many examples of high-profile organizations that have failed to identify fundamental external shifts and challenges to their business model and suffered serious consequences as a result. It is a myth to assume that flexible working is only suitable for some roles and not others.

Flexible working is a women's (or a mothers') issue

The history of flexible working and its original conception as a right for parents of young children has to some extent been responsible for the idea that flexible working is for parents, and in particular for mothers returning to work after maternity leave. This narrow focus leads to missed opportunities to use flexible working to meet broader societal and economic goals (Fagan *et al*, 2006).

The evidence that we have already considered has demonstrated that this perception is false. In fact, according to CIPD data from their 2019 *UK Working Lives* research, caring responsibilities were the primary drivers of flexible working for fewer than a quarter of employees (this figure included both caring for children and other relatives). There are, however, a range of societal factors that contribute to the view that flexible working is about childcare. Due to the gender pay gap, women often earn less than their male partner. Therefore, if one parent does wish to reduce their hours following the birth of a child it often follows that it will be the lower earner – usually the mother. Secondly, women still undertake the bulk of domestic labour in the home, including childcare. So whilst flexible working is not necessarily more desired by mothers in terms of personal aims and objectives, and despite research (discussed in Chapter 4) suggesting that many fathers want more flexibility and to be more involved with childcare, it is still often the mothers who are asking for flexible working. The fact that this is the case further perpetuates the problem: fathers who want to work flexibly are not seen as the norm, presenting even bigger barriers for them when they wish to do so.

Unfortunately, many fathers report similar challenges as those experienced by working mothers. A 2019 survey found that 2 in 5 fathers have had their requests for flexible working turned down, and 1 in 5 who do work flexibly feel discriminated against by their managers and colleagues (*People Management*, 2019). A 2019 Deloitte survey of 3,000 fathers found that one-third of fathers of young children were looking to move employers to find a role with greater flexibility to allow them to spend more time with their children (Deloitte, 2019).

The myth that flexible working is primarily for parents can also be challenged by the positioning of an organization's flexible working policy. The Family and Childcare Trust warned (in a report to the Women and Equalities Committee) that 'flexible working practices can become stigmatized if they are promoted solely as an option for parents and carers' (2016). Instead of including flexible working policies with information and communications about 'family-friendly' benefits, flexible working policies must be positioned as available for all staff.

From a policy point of view, it is not unusual to find that a flexible working policy (or standard application form) asks employees to state their reason for wishing to work flexibly as part of the application process. It is likely that this practice dates back to the previous legislative framework where flexible working requests were only available to parents and carers. This policy requirement is problematic for several reasons. Firstly, it invites a value judgement on the part of the manager considering the request. Is it, for example, more desirable to say yes to a request from a carer rather than from an individual who wishes to reduce their commuting time or pursue a course of study? Is one request more 'worthy' than another? Secondly, this approach suggests that the reason for requesting flexibility is somehow relevant to the decision as to whether or not it can be approved. It can in turn lead to a discussion about whether the employee is required to 'prove' this need. There should be no hierarchy when it comes to the desire for and receipt of flexible working. If we accept that flexible working can lead to benefits for both individuals and organizations alike, there should be no requirement for employees to specify their reasons for wanting to undertake it. This is essentially another part of necessary reframing – supporting employees to work flexibly because they want to, rather than because they need to. Where policies or forms have such a process requirement, its removal is recommended.

Flexible working is a subject that is replete with myths, and workers who undertake flexible working are often subject to negative stereotypes. These myths contribute to the complex picture of flexible working in the UK. Just like the barriers discussed in the previous chapter, myths get in the way of acceptance and adoption. Myths can be dismantled, but it will take time, evidence and concerted action from multiple stakeholders. When we succeed, everyone benefits.

If you find yourself up against these myths in your workplace, you can use the evidence and information relating to flexible working from Chapters 2, 3 and 4 to help you to rebut them.

In the next chapter we will explore another topic that presents a challenge to a more flexible future: the barriers to effective flexible working and operating against flexible workers themselves.

KEY TAKEAWAYS

- Flexible working is associated with numerous myths, many of which can form a barrier to the acceptance and success of flexible working.

- Some of these myths are related to stereotypes and unconscious biases.

- Some of these myths relate to beliefs about flexible workers themselves, and others relate to the operation of flexible working arrangements.

- Many of the myths associated with flexible working do not stand up to scrutiny and lack an evidence base; they can, however, be difficult to change and will require ongoing effort from organizations.

- Some myths may be specific to particular organizations; it can be helpful to understand what myths about flexible working are prevalent in any one business in addition to those more commonly found.

References

Berkun, S (2013) *The Year without Pants*, Jossey-Bass, San Francisco, CA

Chung, H (2018) Gender, Flexibility stigma and the perceived negative consequences of flexible working in the UK, *Social Indicators Research*, doi.org/10.1007/s11205-018-2036-7 (archived at https://perma.cc/X2SU-VXBG)

Chung, H and van der Lippe, T (2018) Flexible working: Work life balance and gender equality, *Social Indicators Research*, doi.org/10.1007/s11205-018-2025-x (archived at https://perma.cc/78H2-YT94)

CIPD (2019) *Working Lives Survey*, Wheatley, D and Gifford, J, CIPD, London

Deloitte (2019) *The Millennial Dad at Work Report*, in association with Daddilife, www.daddilife.com/wp-content/uploads/2019/05/The-Millenial-Dad-at-Work-Report-2019.pdf (archived at https://perma.cc/K8MV-NSSH)

Fagan, C, Hegewisch, A and Pillinger, J (2006) *Out of Time: Why Britain needs a new approach to working-time flexibility*, Trades Union Congress, www.researchgate.net/publication/286447808_Out_of_Time_-_why_Britain_needs_a_new_approach_to_working-time_flexibility (archived at https://perma.cc/B87P-XQRV)

Kelliher, C and Anderson, D (2010) *Doing More With Less? Flexible working practices and the intensification of work*, The Tavistock Institute

Mullins, L (2016) *Management and Organizational Behaviour*, 11th edn, Pearson

People Management (2019) Fathers struggle to get the flexible work they need, says survey, *People Management*, www.peoplemanagement.co.uk/news/articles/fathers-struggle-to-get-flexible-work (archived at https://perma.cc/Y5YE-JSAB)

TUC (2019) *A Four-Day Week With Decent Pay For All? It's the future*, www.tuc.org.uk/blogs/four-day-week-decent-pay-all-its-future (archived at https://perma.cc/NE3C-BME9)

Wheatley, D (2012) Work–life balance, travel-to-work and the dual career household, *Personnel Review*, **41**(6)

Wheatley, D and Gifford, J (2019) *Working Lives Survey*, CIPD, www.cipd.co.uk/Images/uk-working-lives-2019-v1_tcm18-58585.pdf (archived at https://perma.cc/TX9A-5S83)

Women and Equalities Committee Report (2016) *Gender Pay Gap*, House of Commons, publications.parliament.uk/pa/cm201516/cmselect/cmwomeq/584/584.pdf (archived at https://perma.cc/6TAU-X4KQ)

07

The barriers to flexible working, and how to overcome them

Chapter 6 explored the complex mix of myths associated with flexible working and flexible workers themselves. As well as these, there are also multiple (and sometimes interconnected) barriers to the effective application of flexible working at an organizational level, as well as its broader acceptance in the corporate world. According to CIPD research, the most commonly cited barriers to the use of flexible working arrangements are: the nature of work that employees do at their organization (27 per cent); negative attitudes from senior managers (15 per cent); and negative attitudes from supervisors and line managers (14 per cent) (CIPD, 2016).

Some of the barriers to flexible working are related to practical issues, whereas others are perceived or attitudinal. Fundamentally, many of the barriers that exist are cultural. Some of them are fairly typical to many organizations, but others are specific to the particular context, industry or role types. Through the identification of barriers, it becomes possible to plan strategies and take action in order to overcome or mitigate them – where an organization sufficiently desires to do so. This chapter will explore some of the main barriers and challenges relating to the adoption and acceptance of flexible working approaches.

Organizational culture

Organizational culture is often explained as 'the way things are done around here'. It is more formally described as the shared values, attitudes, beliefs, experiences and behaviours of both the organization and the people working within it. In every place of work there exist both a formal and an informal organization. The formal aspect of culture is what we see in designed structures, policies and strategies. It is what is espoused. Alongside it, and always present, sits the informal organization. It is comprised of informal communication channels, personal relationships, informal leaders, stories and feelings. The informal organization is not designed or deliberate. It emerges naturally, and sometimes in spite of or in contrast to its formal counterpart. Flexible working as an idea and approach will exist in both, and therefore it is necessary to pay attention to the needs and operations of these two elements when we want to influence them.

Culture is highly influential upon how change is received and takes place – as well as whether it is ultimately successful. Culture can be notoriously difficult to change – but not impossible. We will return to this subject later when we discuss implementation of flexible working strategies. In relation specifically to flexible working, according to a global survey by the International Workplace Group (2019), 60 per cent of respondents said that changing long-standing, non-flexible organization cultures is an obstacle to introducing flexible working.

Even when formal change is attempted, sometimes the informal aspects of culture impede its progress. There can be a tension between what an organization says is its culture (or what it wants it to be) and what is experienced by employees on a day-to-day basis. The culture of an organization influences how work is done in practice. Consider, for example, how people get together to collaborate or make decisions. For many organizations and teams, a face-to-face meeting is the default approach. The relevant people will all gather in one room, regardless of how long it takes for each participant to travel there or how convenient the location is. A discussion will take place, actions will be agreed and the participants will each return to their work stations. Although there are undoubtedly good reasons for teams to get together in person, it is not always necessary for meetings to take place in this way, but they often continue to do so because that is the prevailing culture – the way things are done around here. Technology has provided us with many alternatives to face-to-face meetings, from online collaboration spaces (reducing the need for real-time discussion at all) or meetings via video-conference or applications like Skype. Although much of this technology has been available for some years now, the culture of the organization may not yet have adopted it. The issue is therefore not one of simply availability or access (Skype can be accessed from any laptop or mobile) but adoption and tradition (culture). We can see therefore that organizational culture can provide a barrier in and of itself.

Attitudes and beliefs are part of organizational culture. As we have already seen, there are unfortunately many negative perceptions of and associations with flexible working. Some of these are the myths that we considered in Chapter 6. Too often, managers and organizations conflate being present with being productive; seeing is therefore managing. This in turn leads to a particular, and deeply damaging, cultural problem in its own right: presenteeism. 'Presenteeism' is being physically present at work, possibly for longer than is required either by the contract of employment or what is necessary to complete the required duties, largely for the purposes of being seen to be at work, as it is understood that this is what is valued. It can also include attending work whilst unwell. Closely related to presenteeism is another concept referred to as 'leavism': working whilst on leave or other allocated time off, sometimes in order to keep up with a high workload. The term can be used to refer to the practice of using annual leave instead of taking time off work whilst unwell.

Presenteeism and leavism can arise within organizational cultures for a variety of reasons: they may be related to fears about job security, it can be seen as culturally unacceptable to leave 'on time' or simply switch off, or they can be (real or perceived) routes to promotion or reward. In some organizations it is assumed that people who are in the office for long hours are therefore more productive or committed to their role or to the organization itself. This may or may not be true. It could be equally possible that someone working long hours is struggling to cope, has an inappropriate workload or too few resources. However, if being present is seen as good (and even rewarded) in a particular organizational culture the flexible worker will be at a particular disadvantage. This is sometimes referred to as 'flexism': a particular form of discrimination or disadvantage through which flexible workers are subject to negative views about their level of commitment or motivation, or perceptions that they do not want to pursue career development or progression. This may arise as outright discrimination (reduced opportunities for learning and development, refusal to consider flexible workers for promotion) or in other, more insidious forms. Stories that people are subject to inappropriate forms of 'banter' are common, as well as dismissive forms of language such as referring to an individual as '*only working part-time*'.

There is no evidence to suggest that employees who work flexibly will be less productive, committed or competent. In fact, research by Working Families in 2018 found that a comparison of performance review ratings for part-time staff outweighed those of their full-time contemporaries. The percentage of top performance ratings for part-time and reduced-hours workers was higher than the percentage of top performance ratings when compared with all staff, at 34 per cent against 14 per cent respectively (Working Families, 2018). This is not the only evidence to rebut this outdated viewpoint. Researchers at the University of Manchester also found that employees who work flexibly often have greater levels of commitment and willingness to 'give back' to their organizations and flexible arrangements can therefore work as a motivator (Clarke and Holdsworth, 2017).

The availability of evidence to counteract negative views of flexible workers will not, however, prevent such attitudes from arising. As already discussed in Chapter 2, research conducted by Chung (2018) examined flexibility stigma in detail, exploring perceptions that flexible workers were less committed or less productive. Results showed that 35 per cent of all workers agreed with the statement that 'those who work flexibly create more work for others'; whilst 32 per cent believed that those who worked flexibly had 'lower chances for promotion'. These findings were highly gendered: more men were likely to discriminate against flexible workers and more women (particularly mothers) were likely to experience it. These findings indicate that many organizations have a long way to go before flexible forms of work are normalized and accepted. Changing attitudes may be a lengthy and complex process.

Trust is one more cultural issue – and a potentially significant barrier to the adoption of flexible working. As already identified, trust is a fundamental element to enable flexibility. Flexible working is built on trust – the idea that people will do their best even when they are not physically present in a particular location or under direct supervision. This is the very opposite of those cultures in which presenteeism and leavism thrive. CIPD research found that 13 per cent of employees say that their organization has a culture that places an emphasis on being seen at their desk (CIPD, 2016). This is a perception that must be challenged if flexible working is to thrive – if there is to be a real flexible working revolution. Being seen to be present is, of course, meaningless; it is not an indicator of capability, competence or productivity.

In practical terms the absence of trust will lead to the rejection of individual flexible working applications and the failure to reap the potential of increased flexibility in general. Some forms of flexible working are more likely to raise trust issues in managers who are resistant to flexible working. For example, someone undertaking a job-share is also working flexibly but may well be still in the office during 'normal' business hours, putting in 'face time'. A homeworker, in contrast, requires significant amounts of trust from a manager, as they are not physically present. This is just one more example where the form of flexibility undertaken has an impact on availability and outcomes.

There are, however, some organizations who know that where culture is focused on flexibility and trust, benefits can flow.

CASE STUDY
Boo Coaching and Consulting

Leadership development and coaching specialist Boo Coaching and Consulting was established with flexibility in mind.

Founder Becci Martin intended Boo to be an organization that could add social value to the community alongside its corporate aims and would also be somewhere that people would want to work – a different kind of environment. This included being a place that would also be free of the rules and regulations she had experienced in corporate life that so often frustrate employees.

At Boo, there is no such thing as 'standard hours'. The team undertake a range of working patterns. Some employees work full-time but have non-standard start and finish times. Others work hours spread throughout the week or year, often around childcare availability, and some of the team combine working with Boo part-time with other work or studies.

Boo has an employee handbook that talks about flexible working and invites employees to 'talk to us about what works for you'. Most discussions about working hours simply take place through conversations, not formal processes. When working directly with clients delivering coaching or development programmes, Boo's team will work the hours that meet the needs of their client. When not undertaking client-facing work, the team can work from anywhere and mostly set their own schedules. The exception is that once a month all members of the team get together for a day at their head office in Bolton, where they connect and have lunch together. When working remotely, the team organize their work by using shared calendars so everyone knows when and where the rest of the team are working should they need to contact each other. Everyone has the technology they need to work remotely – and there is no clocking in or clocking out. Even 121s can take place virtually.

Martin is keen to point out that being present does not equal being productive. Her philosophy is to let people work in a way that works for them and meets their personal needs; where people can come to work and be authentically themselves as this will lead to employees who are healthier and happier, for whom work does not feel like a chore. Ultimately everyone benefits from flexibility: employees, clients and Boo itself.

Framing

Aside from organization culture, the biggest barrier of all of those discussed here is perhaps the failure to see the broader picture of flexibility and its place in the future of work. Flexible working is often seen both by individual managers and organizations in general as an employee benefit. It is not the norm, but an exception to it. Interestingly, even the government's own definition of flexible is 'a form of working that suits an employee's needs' (www.gov.uk (archived at https://perma.cc/4TVM-ZXGE)). It therefore becomes individualized in nature. As we have seen, this is often narrowed even further by positioning it not necessarily as a benefit for all staff but as a benefit mostly for working parents, or, even more narrowly again, for working mothers of young children. This narrative fails to acknowledge the extensive benefits of flexible working to the whole organization that were explored in Chapter 2. Where the organization (and its managers) frames flexible working as primarily an employee benefit, it may lead to managers perceiving flexible working as leading to a loss (or worse, a cost) for the organization. Flexible working therefore becomes a one-way benefit lacking in reciprocity. This is a fundamental error and tackling it requires significant reframing at all levels if flexible working is to be accepted.

In 2011, the then Coalition government set up a taskforce comprising 21 large organizations across multiple sectors to look at flexible working practices in the UK and how these might be developed and increased. This taskforce was chaired by Sir Winfried Bischoff, Chairman of Lloyds Banking Group, and was initially named the 'Employers Group on Workforce Flexibility'. A recognition of the negative associations attached to flexible working, some of which are discussed in the forthcoming chapter, led to that group renaming itself the 'Agile Working Forum' in 2013. 'Agile' is of course a much more attractive term, bringing with it entirely different connotations. Agility sounds much more desirable, much more business-focused – and something that we might want our employees to *be* rather than *do*. This change was seen as a significant turning point for the group, without which its efforts may have stalled – it suddenly became about how organizations could enhance their competitiveness (Cannon and Elford, 2017).

In order to persuade an organization of the benefits of flexible working it may be necessary to rethink the language that we use, the overall positioning of flexibility, and undertake a campaign of education. Drawing on the example from the Agile Futures Forum, how we frame flexible working to managers, leaders and the wider organization may ultimately influence its success (or otherwise).

One alternative approach to overcoming the framing and positioning barrier is for an organization to take a proactive and business-wide stance on flexibility, and introduce what is sometimes referred to as 'flexible working by default'. This changes the approach from flexible working being something that is asked for by an individual to something that is automatically available for all employees (and potentially job applicants). Whereas the current model effectively requires the employee to consider how flexible working can be effective on an individual and case-by-case basis, 'flexible by default' starts from the position of assuming that it will. Under this scheme the onus is placed on a manager (or recruiting manager) to put together a case to justify why flexible working would not be suitable, and this business case would be subject to scrutiny. This innovative approach challenges the traditional way of doing things and can help overcome multiple barriers, including many of those discussed in this chapter. It may not, however, if adopted, be popular with people managers.

Flexible by default is not commonplace, but some organizations are implementing it. One such organization is the University of Sussex, who announced their adoption of this model in 2018. They position their approach to flexible working as central to creating an environment of equality, diversity and inclusion. They state in their flexible working guidance, 'all positions will be advertised as suitable for flexible working by default, unless a clear business case can be made for not doing so'.

Managers

People managers will, in most organizations, be the individuals responsible for considering and approving or rejecting individual requests for flexible working. By virtue of their position, they have significant influence over the culture of the organization, both formally and informally, and therefore whether flexible working is not only allowed on an individual basis but more widely accepted. Research by the Royal Society of Arts (RSA) in 2013 found that many managers were 'lukewarm' to flexible working, with 53 per cent of employees describing a culture of tolerance through to active discouragement (19 per cent) (RSA, 2013).

Some managers are reluctant to support flexible working applications for a range of reasons. These reasons may be related to some of those flexible working myths identified in Chapter 6, such as concerns about setting precedents or flexible workers being more difficult to manage, or a belief that those working flexibly will be less committed or motivated. They may be concerned about productivity, additional costs, impact on quality of work or even discontent from others in their team. Managers, of course, will be highly influenced by both the organizational culture in which they operate as well as the leaders more senior to them and their attitudes to flexibility. This complex mix of beliefs, attitudes and influences can lead in some organizations to what the Government Equalities Office refers to as a flexible working 'line manager lottery' (Nicks *et al*, 2019). The manager is usually the best person to understand if a job can be undertaken flexibly, and therefore they play a key role in the process – but there is a risk that decisions will be made based on irrelevant factors. How liked is the employee? To what extent are they seen as valuable and therefore important to retain? What is their personal level of performance? Here lies the challenge for an organization and its human resources function – ensuring that managers can apply their knowledge fairly and appropriately and without recourse to unrelated factors.

Flexible working is a process prescribed for by legislation and this can further add to its poor reputation. The ability to request flexible working is a legal right, with a specified formal process. This can in its own right have an unintended consequence, bringing with it undertones of something a manager *must* do; a duty to be addressed and a (potentially) lengthy process to follow. The wider context of both the benefits of flexibility and the broader context of flexibility, and the changing nature of work are lost in the application of policy and process.

Reluctance to embrace flexible working may not only be an issue of attitude but also one of skills. Many managers rely primarily on face-to-face contact with their employees as their default management technique. They will typically have traditional ways of working for both them and their team which could be disrupted by someone who wants to work differently. For some managers, this may feel like a threat, leading to a defensive position. Managing flexible workers may require a different (although not necessarily more difficult) approach and managers may need support in developing these skills as an organization moves towards a more flexible approach. A study by Henley Management College called *Managing Tomorrow's Worker* found that managing flexible workers tends to lead to a higher demand for some leadership skills, including communication, team-building, decision-making and coaching when compared to managing workers undertaking more traditional patterns of work; equipping managers to work in a more flexible future therefore requires more than an information session on the legislation and policy (Henley Management College, 2005). Managers of remote teams also need to rethink how they assess and measure productivity and performance, as well as ensuring that there is effective socialization with the business for remote workers (Cooper and Hesketh, 2019).

Lack of senior leadership buy-in can be an additional issue to overcome within individual organizations. Senior leaders may themselves suffer from some of the same biases identified as those held by other people managers. They may not appreciate the business benefits of flexibility or may be concerned about potential negative implications for the organization. The second way in which senior leaders can amount to a barrier is through a lack of leaders who are visibly working flexibly themselves. This can help to perpetuate myths that flexible working is not possible for senior roles, or is not approved of. The first step to tackling this particular barrier is the development of a compelling business case, combined with a practical, operational plan that will help to reduce any potential concerns about implementation or implications. This will be explored in more detail later.

Awareness raising and specific training can be helpful in reassuring managers and supporting them in developing new skills. For example, if a manager does rely on casual contact with their team for the purposes of communication, they may need to think about putting in a schedule of regular 121s instead. Training provided to people managers should include the statutory framework, guidance on the management of applications (including how to assess roles for suitability), the benefits of flexible working, and tips for the management of flexible workers, as well as the broader context and development of different leadership skills.

Some managers will simply need to know what is in it for them when it comes to flexible working. The role that the HR professional can play is particularly important in articulating these benefits in the specific context within which they are operating.

The flexibility stigma

As we have already seen, negative attitudes towards flexible working persist, and consequently stigma is a barrier to flexible working in many ways.

Stigma appears in workplaces in many forms: through direct and indirect discrimination, through 'banter', career stagnation, reduced opportunities and poor working relationships.

Stigma exists as a barrier to seeking flexibility when employees believe that their careers will be negatively impacted by doing so, either in terms of future promotion or progression. Women and mothers are more likely to agree with those negative statements about career progression and say that they experienced negative consequences themselves from working flexibly. This is likely to be related to the fact that mothers are most likely to use forms of flexibility where hours are reduced, such as part-time work (Chung and van der Lippe, 2018). Generally speaking, it is women who fear the consequences of flexible working, and who are more likely to experience them (Chung, 2018).

Stigma also exists as a barrier to job applicants, who fear that their application will be treated less favourably if they raise a question during recruitment and selection activity.

Finally, stigma also acts as a barrier to effective working relationships as well as the acceptance of individual requests. A significant number of people believe that flexible workers create work for other people and that flexible workers have less chance of promotion. In 2013 the RSA published a research paper called *The Flex Factor*. They segmented employees by their attitudes to flexible working, and identified two groups whose attitudes to flexible working were largely negative and unlikely to shift easily: traditionalists and sceptics. They described the traditionalist as someone who prefers standard hours of work, likes routine and defined working patterns. The sceptic has negative perceptions about flexible working, avoids change and prefers the status quo (RSA, 2013). Some of these individuals will undoubtedly also be in managerial roles. These are individuals whom we can easily recognize; many of us could perhaps identify people within our own organizations fitting these broad descriptions. Working with these groups, especially when they are also managers or even senior leaders (discussed later), will be challenging but ultimately essential to the acceptance of flexible forms of working.

Colleagues

On occasions, flexible working can cause friction between colleagues. An 'it's alright for some' attitude is often reported by those who work flexibly.

Flexible workers also report themselves as being on the receiving end of workplace 'banter' about their hours of work. This can be a particular issue in organizations where the opportunity for flexible working is applied inconsistently, or the personal beliefs and attitudes of particular managers are at the heart of decision-making about flexibility. It may also be a particular issue when flexible working is relatively new to an organization or specific team, or when only one person is working differently to the majority of their colleagues. Flexibility stigma can arise from colleagues too, not just managers.

Working flexibly, particularly remotely, can also have an impact on connectedness: the extent to which workers feel connected to their colleagues. When the majority of a team works standard hours and one or two individuals work flexibly, it can from time to time lead to those individuals feeling excluded. According to research by flexible working company Timewise, two-thirds of part-time workers feel isolated and less connected to their own teams and they find it difficult to make professional connections. Deliberate strategies to address this barrier can be simply employed by people managers; ensuring remote workers are not forgotten or left out is a matter for good communication and a little effort (Timewise, 2018).

Organizations must take a zero-tolerance approach to inappropriate behaviour towards flexible workers, in the same way that they would any other type of exclusionary behaviour. Manager training can highlight the potential for this issue to arise – as well as their responsibility in addressing it.

Consistency of policy application

Having a well-written and communicated policy is a key element of enabling a flexible workplace. This is, however, only the starting point; that policy also needs to be well understood and applied in practice. Another regular barrier identified to flexible working is the extent to which organizations apply their policy inconsistently, or, whilst a policy exists, employees are discouraged from using it through a variety of means. It is a common complaint, especially in larger organizations, that what is permitted or even encouraged in one department or team is expressly forbidden in others. This can be a result of the views of individual managers and their personal beliefs about flexible working.

The barrier is a practical one and is a real issue for many employees, and has the potential to lead to a loss of engagement and possibly even increase the number of grievances raised. Whilst there can never be complete consistency in outcome (there will always be requests that cannot be accommodated), an organization can aim to achieve parity of process and a reasonable consideration of all requests.

Ensuring consistency of policy application is partly a function of the human resources department. This can be supported by the provision of learning and development for managers, identifying potential issues by taking feedback from employees and monitoring data on applications and their outcomes. Where issues are identified through data analysis, proactive interventions must be made. This can be a challenge for some organizations, however, as HR may not have full visibility of all requests.

In a large organization with multiple job types, it is inevitable that there will be some functions and departments in which the potential for flexible working is more limited than in others. What can appear to be an inconsistency in application or a 'problem area' may in fact be an implementation issue and it is important to distinguish between the two.

Ensuring consistency, combined with clear communication when different approaches are taken, is key if employees are to feel that the overall approach to flexible working is fair and reasonable.

Human resources

In the worst case scenario the HR function can amount to a barrier to flexible working in its own right. Exactly how this barrier manifests itself will vary according to the organization. It may be that the HR department has written an ineffective or overly restrictive policy or process. Alternatively, HR professionals may themselves fail to understand the organizational benefits to flexible working, thereby aligning with the narrative that flexible working is a cost or represents a loss to the business. Finally, they may collude with managers and support them in finding ways to say no to individual requests. This is not true of all HR professionals; many of them will understand and articulate the benefits of flexibility to managers and the wider organization and lead for change, as well as challenge outdated attitudes when they identify them.

An effective HR function will enable flexible working, understand its implications beyond working parents, and provide effective challenge to managers who take a negative approach to new ways of working. They will also be capable of tailoring flexible working approaches to suit their own organization's specific context, as well as identifying good practice in other organizations and sharing that internally. In order for HR to fulfil this responsibility, they may also require specific training and development. It is not sufficient for HR professionals to simply understand and be able to advise on the relevant legislation; if they really want to support their organization in being fit for the future then HR must take their own learning and awareness to a deeper level. HR departments can help to develop a culture in which flexible working can thrive – if they choose to do so.

The statutory framework

As already discussed in Chapter 1, UK legislation governing flexible working provides for a minimum length of service (26 weeks) before an employee can make a request for flexible working. The same legislation also sets out a process for employers to follow in relation to the consideration of this request – and this can take up to a maximum of three months.

Underlying this time period is an implication that flexible working needs to be 'earned'. It begins from a position of low trust. Whilst we have supposedly identified an individual as the best person for a given job role following a (presumably) robust recruitment and selection process, they still need to somehow prove themselves further before they can be considered suitable to undertake modern working practices, or work without direct supervision. These two ideas contradict each other.

The UK legislation was designed to support flexible working, but the framework presents a considerable practical barrier in its own right, particularly in relation to the acquisition of talent. Where employers require new starters to wait to request flexible working, potential recruits may never opt to even apply for the role. Individuals who already work flexibly at a current employer may be disinclined to apply for a role where they would not be able to even ask for flexible working arrangements for six months – and take the risk of being turned down. The alternative solution would be to apply for the role, find temporary workarounds for six months if appointed, and hope for the best for a future application – a situation many would not consider feasible or practicable.

Some employers have recognized this problem and have implemented improved policies that allow for employees to make a request from 'Day One' of employment, or even during the recruitment period, actively promoting this opportunity in recruitment advertising. This can either be through a simple strapline such as the Working Families' 'happy to talk flexible working' example or more detailed information on the forms of flexible working the organization would be willing to consider for the particular vacancy being advertised. Both the potential employee and their manager would benefit from a conversation about working patterns at the earliest possible stage in the process – not in six months' time – and such policy approaches facilitate this. By introducing policy that supports employees applying for flexible working from Day One of employment, advertising vacancies as open to considering flexible working and equipping managers to have these conversations during the recruitment process, employers can reduce the barriers inherent in the statutory process.

A further issue in the drafting of the legislation which also represents a barrier to accessing flexible working is the provision that employees can only make one request in a rolling 12-month period. The intention of this clause was to ensure that employers were not subject to multiple requests from individuals which would be time-consuming and unhelpful. However, it is entirely feasible that life circumstances may change dramatically over the course of a year and so, therefore, might the need for an amended working pattern. This is a minor point but can still be a practical issue for some employees. This can be overcome through amending policy to provide for management discretion in such situations.

Technology

Technology enables not only flexible working but new ways of working, even for those who continue to undertake more traditional patterns of work. Most of the technology required to work flexibly is readily available in almost all organizations. Many organizations use cloud-based software and that, along with a wifi connection, is all that is required for effective work for a great many occupations. Our changing types of work have also reduced the need for some aspects of work to be synchronous. However, just because the technology exists does not mean that individuals are able to use it effectively. Capability in relation to technology can also be a potential significant barrier. The homeworker may be effective with a range of online tools, but if their colleagues are unable (or simply unwilling) to use them this may present a further barrier to effective flexible working. Therefore, technology on its own is not an enabler of flexible working – it also requires that technology to be understood, accepted and used.

Technology adoption can be driven by a number of factors, including how easy it is to use and for people to feel that there is a compelling reason to do so. Even when a flexible worker is able to fully undertake their role through using technology, where their colleagues are unable to engage with them remotely or through various forms of technology, the success of the flexible working arrangement will be negatively impacted. Even if the technology is easy, colleagues may not feel that they need to engage with it to support a flexible working colleague.

Although this chapter details many barriers to flexible working, none of them are insurmountable where there is the commitment, and potentially available resources, to overcome them. This is not to suggest that overcoming them will be quick or easy: culture is difficult to change and influence and so are the beliefs and attitudes of individuals. Tackling the barriers is, however, essential for the successful adoption of flexible working. Doing so is a combined responsibility between human resources, leaders, managers and flexible workers themselves. In particular, flexible workers can help to educate and influence others.

As we continue through this book we will return to some of the barriers discussed in this chapter in more depth and how we might tackle them through effective implementation of flexible working strategies and approaches.

KEY TAKEAWAYS

- There are many barriers to flexible working. These can generally be divided into practical barriers (such as the availability of technology) or attitude- and belief-based barriers (such as people's perceptions of flexible workers).

- Barriers can work hand in hand with myths about flexible work and workers, amounting together to a significant obstacle to flexible working adoption.

- Barriers can be general in nature or specific to an organization's own particular context – organizations should consider which barriers apply to their own unique situation as part of their implementation strategy.

- If barriers are not identified and tackled, they will prevent the benefits of flexibility from being fully realized and have a negative impact on individual flexible workers.

- Addressing these complex issues may not be quick or easy, but there is much that organizations can do to tackle barriers to effective flexible working. Barriers are rarely insurmountable.

References

Cannon, F and Elford, N (2017) *The Agility Mindset: How reframing flexible working delivers competitive advantage*, Palgrave Macmillan, Switzerland

Chung, H (2018) Gender, flexibility stigma and the perceived negative consequences of flexible working in the UK, *Social Indicators Research*, doi.org/10.1007/s11205-018-2036-7 (archived at https://perma.cc/X2SU-VXBG)

Chung, H and van der Lippe, T (2018) Flexible working, work life balance and gender equality, *Social Indicators Research*, doi.org/10.1007/s11205-018-2025-x (archived at https://perma.cc/78H2-YT94)

CIPD (2016) *Employee Outlook, Employee Views on Working Life: Focus on commuting and flexible working*, CIPD, London, www.cipd.co.uk/Images/employee-outlook-focus-on-commuting-and-flexible-working_tcm18-10886.pdf (archived at https://perma.cc/G8WM-LLF8)

Clarke, S and Holdsworth, L (2017) *Flexibility in the Workplace: Implications of flexible working arrangements for individuals, teams and organizations*, Acas, archive.acas.org.uk/media/4901/Flexibility-in-the-Workplace-Implications-of-flexible-work-arrangements-for-individuals-teams-and-organizations/pdf/Flexibility-in-the-Workplace.pdf (archived at https://perma.cc/52XB-KTJ7)

Cooper, C and Hesketh, I (2019) *Wellbeing at Work: How to design, implement and evaluate an effective strategy*, Kogan Page, London

Henley Management College (2005) *Managing Tomorrow's Worker*, download.microsoft.com/documents/uk/business/reality/ManagingTomorrowsWorker.pdf (archived at https://perma.cc/SM2D-NTLL)

International Workplace Global Workplace Survey (2019) *Welcome to Generation Flex: The employee power shift*, assets.regus.com/pdfs/iwg-workplace-survey/iwg-workplace-survey-2019.pdf (archived at https://perma.cc/PR9P-84RE)

Nicks, L, Burd, H and Barnes, J (2019) *Flexible Working Qualitative Analysis: Organizations' experiences of flexible working arrangements*, Government Equalities Office, assets.publishing.service.gov.uk/government/uploads/system/uploads/attachment_data/file/790354/Flexible-working-qualitative-analysis2.pdf (archived at https://perma.cc/T785-L3DK)

RSA (2013) *The Flex Factor: Realizing the value of flexible working*, www.thersa.org/globalassets/pdfs/blogs/rsa_flex_report_15072013.pdf (archived at https://perma.cc/V4SA-MLMT)

Timewise (2018) *Part-time Work: The exclusion zone*, timewise.co.uk/wp-content/uploads/2018/09/Part-Time_Work_Exclusion_Zone.pdf (archived at https://perma.cc/8NGL-YNVG)

UK government: definition of flexible working: www.gov.uk/flexible-working (archived at https://perma.cc/L4FU-6FM3)

University of Sussex (2018) *Embracing the University's Flexible Working Procedure*, www.sussex.ac.uk/webteam/gateway/file.php?name=flexible-sussex---embracing-the-universitys-flexible-working-procedure.pdf&site=302 (archived at https://perma.cc/99LZ-FES4)

Working Families (2018) *The Modern Families Index 2018*, www.workingfamilies.org.uk/wp-content/uploads/2018/01/UK_MFI_2018_Long_Report_A4_UK.pdf (archived at https://perma.cc/G857-D3E4)

Introducing flexible working

The practical guide

Part One of this book reviewed the broader case for and evidence relating to flexible working, drawing on a range of research, surveys and thinking from leading professionals. It aimed to set the scene as to why flexible working is a critical business issue and how it can help us to tackle some of our current major workplace challenges, from inclusion to corporate social responsibility. It also explained that it is not a panacea, a quick fix or without its challenges. Flexible working causes us to question some of our most fundamental ideas about work and workplaces.

Having set out both the benefits and challenges, Part Two of this book will now turn to the practicalities of successful flexible working implementation. It assumes that an organization wishes to embrace a more flexible future and therefore requires the development of a strategy and approach for adoption.

As such, this section begins by setting out the necessary fundamentals of a flexible workplace in which flexible forms of working can flourish, as well as deliver the potential benefits explored in Part One. These are the flexible working building blocks. There are six elements of a truly flexible organization, some of which we will explore in more depth throughout Part Two of this book, as well as guidance on how they might be achieved.

This section of the book will explore building a business case for flexible working, effective policy development and further steps to ensure that the organization is ready to move towards a more flexible future. It will consider how to communicate your flexible working strategy as well as how to effectively measure the progress and success of flexible working initiatives.

Finally, a detailed tools section will provide a range of sample guidance documents for both employees and people managers that readers can adapt for their own purposes. These tools include a frequently asked questions (FAQ) document and examples of drafting for job advertisements and policy clauses.

08

From compliance to culture

Six elements of a truly flexible workplace

So far, we have explored the potential benefits of flexible working, alongside the barriers, challenges and myths associated with it. For those who are persuaded that it is truly time for a flexible working revolution, we will now turn to the practicalities of achieving it. In order for an organization to fully embrace flexible working and harness its many benefits, there are a number of key elements that must already exist within the organization or be consciously developed in partnership between (typically) senior leaders and the human resources team. These key elements are the foundations for flexibility and a series of aspirations to be met by the organization who wants to move from flexible working compliance (with the minimum standards of the law) to a truly flexible culture. They are the foundations too for organizations who want to move from flexibility being merely tolerated to one in which it is actually celebrated, and which progresses beyond the working parent and carer stereotype. Only by changing cultures can we address some of the deeper issues that are associated with flexible working, and make flexibility the norm and not the exception.

The six elements

1 Flexibility for everyone (or as many people as practicably possible)

There are some job roles and professions where introducing more flexibility is, in theory at least, simple and straightforward, assuming that the organization is willing to move away from the default working model. The type of work that we tend to refer to as 'knowledge work', for example, is perhaps the easiest type of work to be undertaken flexibly. This is, as the term suggests, work that requires specific knowledge and the processing of it. It is work that requires thinking. Examples may include accountants, HR professionals, architects, engineers, writers, marketers, academics or solicitors. This work is potentially flexible in most, if not all, dimensions of when, where and how it is undertaken. Conversely, there are some jobs where it is more difficult, if not impossible, to work flexibly (certainly in the traditional sense of the word). Examples include work where a physical presence is required at particular times, such as retail work in a high-street store, providing catering, security work or a school teaching. It is all too easy to assume a binary situation in which some roles can be suitable for flexible working and some roles are not. Sometimes, these decisions are about seniority: flexible working arrangements are based on grade or hierarchy, as opposed to the nature of the work undertaken. In some organizations, the ability to work flexibly is seen as a perk or part of the benefits package.

Although flexible working options in some roles are inevitably more restricted (homeworking is not going to be available, for example, where a physical presence is required at a particular time) this does not mean that there is *no* possible flexibility. These roles may not lend themselves to all forms of flexible working, but some could be accommodated. For example, job-sharing or self-rostering are examples of how an organization can provide employees with a greater degree of autonomy in relation to working patterns, even if they cannot be flexible on where and how the work is undertaken. A truly flexible organization will reject arbitrary ideas about who can work flexibly, and will base decisions about working arrangements on evidence. Those organizations that reject flexible working for some people or some role types are seeing flexible working through its most narrow lens. Neither is it acceptable for an organization to say no to some employees because they cannot say yes to others – as the data around talent attraction and retention tells us, this is not a long-term viable option.

Some organizations with this in mind are adopting the idea of 'flexible by default', which starts from the premise that all jobs can be undertaken flexibly – and if someone (such as a people manager) believes they cannot, they must provide appropriate justification as to why this is the case. With creativity and open minds, flexibility may be more feasible than it first might seem – or some might believe.

Where flexibility is available to everyone in the organization (or as many people as possible), this will help to shift the culture and reduce the stigma associated with working flexibly that can arise when it is only undertaken by a small group of individuals (often parents). Where it is not available to all or most employees, organizations run the risk of creating a two-tier workforce of those that can and those that cannot. This will only serve to create tensions between employees and teams and perpetuate some of the barriers discussed in Chapter 7.

True culture change will be enabled if we assume that everyone will, and can, benefit from some degree of flexible working.

2 Acceptance of flexibility in all its forms

As we have already seen, flexible working can take many forms and the idea reaches significantly beyond the typical stereotype of a mother returning from maternity leave. We also know, however, that some of the most popular forms of flexible working, such as part-time working, are those with which we are most familiar. Other perhaps more creative forms, such as compressed hours or nine-day fortnights are significantly less utilized. This may be because organizations and their employees are just not familiar with them, or managers are not clear about how to make them work. Despite the fact that employees can legally make a request for any form of flexible working, it is not unusual to find situations where a certain form of flexible working is discouraged or outright prohibited.

Successful adoption of flexible working will not limit the forms of flexible working that are available to employees, even if they have not been undertaken previously. From part-time to job-share, flexi-time to the nine-day fortnight, a flexible culture exists where employees undertake a wide range of flexible working arrangements and are judged by their outcomes, not their hours of work.

A truly flexible organization will be prepared to consider or trial other forms suggested by employees and experiment with what might be possible, rather than make assumptions about what will work and what will not.

3 High trust

Flexible working is most effective in high-trust environments. Ernest Hemingway said that the best way to find out if you can trust somebody is to trust them. Trust is, however, sadly not always present in organizations or in the relationships between managers and their staff. This is often evidenced by many workplace policies, the tone of which assumes that poor behaviour or exploitation of benefit provision will be inevitable. Unfortunately, there is a tendency within many organizations to conflate presence with performance. Employees who work long hours are presumed to be committed and productive. This is not necessarily accurate and may in fact indicate issues of a more problematic nature. These outdated ideas can lead to presenteeism – attendance at work whilst ill has already been identified as a significant business issue. It is of course more sensible to measure performance based on outputs rather than 'face time'.

Too often in the employment relationship we expect people to earn our trust, rather than begin from this position. We see this in many ways through our people processes. Consider, for example, probation periods for new starters: we like someone so much that we offer them a job, but not without a caveat in case they do not turn out to be everything we had hoped. The same applies with flexible working and the 26-week waiting period. This suggests that we will consider flexible working – but only when the employee has somehow proved themselves to be worthy of it, or trustworthy. This is no way to begin a working relationship.

Many managers who object to flexible working do so because of concerns about how people will be measured and managed and how performance can be assured. Such objections are rooted in lack of trust. The management of flexible workers may require a different approach to the ones which managers have typically relied upon, and success will depend on them starting from a position of trust. Managers may well require training in those additional skills – a subject to which we will return later.

Out of all of the six elements, this is perhaps the one most difficult to achieve in practice. There is no quick operational plan or set of objectives that can establish a culture of trust. You cannot simply tell people to trust others if they do not. It is not too difficult to identify cultures where there is low trust. Signs and signals include excessive rules and regulations, rigid hierarchies, lengthy approval processes, senior leader involvement in minor decisions, excessive emailing and micro-management. Providing flexible working can actually help to build a culture of trust through sending a signal to employees that the organization is willing to empower them to determine the best way for them to work. It also demonstrates that the organization believes its people are capable of working without necessarily requiring close supervision, and that the organization also values outcomes and outputs over face time and the hours completed.

4 Enabling and supportive managers and leaders

Managers and leaders at all levels of the organization are critical enablers in successful flexible working. They can also form a significant barrier if they are not sufficiently accepting of these new ways of working.

Senior leaders can give permission, act as role models and support the overall business case. Line managers have the responsibility of day-to-day policy implementation and the management of requests.

In order to support flexible working it is important that managers at all levels throughout the hierarchy understand it – and in particular the benefits that it can bring to them, the people who work for them and the organization as a whole. In particular, it is critical that managers understand that flexible working is an issue for all employees and not just working parents and carers. Equally, an understanding of the potential challenges will enable strategies to be put in place to maximize the potential for success.

When a manager sees flexible working as an opportunity, as opposed to something to be tolerated, work flexibly themselves and are open-minded to experimenting with new ways of working, they will be able to use flexible working to motivate and engage the people that work for them. Engaging managers on flexible working can require a long-term strategy, a subject we will explore later.

We will discuss in more detail in later chapters the particular actions that can be taken to gain the buy-in of managers to flexible working, and give them the skills that they need to enable it.

5 Effective policy

An effective flexible working policy will have several elements. First of all, it needs to tick all of the relevant compliance boxes and set out the legal framework. It should be easy to understand and be accompanied by useful guidance to support implementation. Wherever possible, it should be tailored to the specific organizational context. Leading policy will go beyond the limits of the statutory framework discussed in Chapter 1.

An effective flexible working policy will support manager discretion and will encourage managers and employees to work together to find solutions. An effective policy will not be aimed at working parents or positioned amongst other family-friendly benefits. It will have a welcoming tone of voice and will not focus primarily on how to turn down a request. It will be accompanied by effective guidance and support on how to apply it in practice.

In a truly flexible organization, awareness of the policy will be high amongst managers and employees alike, and it will be easy to access it. There will not be any penalties or negative consequences from doing so. A good policy will ensure that it is easy to make an application, and will provide for a prompt response; it is a key building block in the introduction of flexibility.

Chapter 10 is dedicated to the development of an effective flexible working policy.

6 Enabling technology

Technology has in recent years fundamentally changed how we work and how we communicate with each other. The capability of technology continues to advance at speed and will undoubtedly continue to disrupt how we work.

Technology can be a critical enabler of flexible working – especially remote or homeworking. It allows employees to be effective anywhere – not just in the office. Where technology does not exist (or is not utilized), flexible workers, particularly remote workers, can be excluded from the workplace. However, it does not follow that organizations need to provide new, expensive or complex technology in order for employees to work flexibly. Most of the tools that people use to get their work done in the office (such as email, internet, instant messaging, document sharing, shared online workspaces and social media sites) are available from any location with an internet connection. This, perhaps more than any other factor, has challenged the default working model. However, having these tools available does not necessarily mean that everyone can use them – or will be willing to do so. Adoption of new technology takes time, and this is partly evidenced by how homeworking is approached by many organizations. Although it is entirely possible for employees to do vast amounts of their work from any location, homeworking is still an exception to the norm and something that employees might do once a week rather than being an integrated way of working.

When it comes to home or remote forms of flexible working, the overall aim for technology must be that employees can have the same levels of access, tools and functionality that they would have in an office environment, subject to appropriate security protocols. For most organizations this is not difficult to achieve from a technological point of view. This is rarely the real barrier – instead, it is a cultural one.

Using technology may mean a shift for some employees in the way they have traditionally worked. For example, the face-to-face meeting is the default in many businesses as a way of getting things done: it does not even seem to matter that most people dislike meetings intensely and they are not generally even that efficient. We continue to have them all the same, because this is what we know. However, a face-to-face meeting is not always neces-sary, and an online conversation can be a more than satisfactory alternative – but it will challenge 'the way we have always done things', to which some people may react poorly. It also means that employees need to know how to hold an online meeting. Therefore, if an organization wishes to drive a cul-ture of flexibility, it will need not only to provide the relevant technology but also ensure that it can be used effectively – not just by the flexible worker but by everyone in the organization. Attention will need to be paid to how technology is adopted and how it is diffused over time.

Together, these six elements will enable change within organizational culture, both its formal and informal aspects. Each of these elements is intercon-nected and mutually supporting; working on them individually will in turn support the other. Without action in each of these areas, the flexible working revolution cannot be fully realized; there will be not so much a revolution as a period of slight turbulence.

The six elements will help an organization to make the transition from one that complies with legislation to one in which flexibility is part of the fabric of the organization – an organization that is fit for the future. Each element must be considered in the strategic plan. These elements are generic; they can apply to all organizations. It may, however, be possible that some organizations will identify their own additional elements that are unique to their sector, job roles, organization type and context.

The following chapters will consider some of these key elements in more detail, providing a range of practical ideas and templates for bringing them to reality.

Changing culture

As we discussed in Chapter 7, organization culture is often described as 'the way things are done around here' – the unwritten rules that are quickly communicated to new team members. It is more formally described as the shared values, attitudes, beliefs, experiences and behaviours of both the organization and the people working within it. We have already identified that having a culture which is negative towards flexible working (or indeed new working practices in general) will be a significant barrier to the adoption of flexible working. We also know that culture is resistant and can be tough to change.

Introducing flexible working, and moving towards implementation of the six elements of a flexible organization, may (depending on the current culture of the organization) demand a significant change in culture. Routinely using technology to communicate, offering whole new ways of working, moving to judging people via results and not time worked, managing people without face-to-face supervision – these are all potentially significant shifts for many organizations and, crucially, their people managers.

How much of a change this amounts to will vary according to the circumstances, and how different working flexibly is from the status quo. How should an organization approach the challenge of culture change? When it comes to introducing flexibility, there is much that we can learn from organizational change models and theory.

People are at the heart of change. Although we often use the term 'organizational change', underneath this is people: their attitudes, beliefs and values. Much organizational change rests on influencing hearts and minds. Many change initiatives and programmes fail or do not work as well as they needed to. There are many reasons why this may be the case. It could be the result of poor planning, a failure to get people to buy into the need for change, employee resistance, or a lack of time or resources assigned to the initiative. One thing is certain: telling people that they need to change and expecting them to do so, even when this communication is delivered by senior leaders, will not lead to a meaningful or sustained change. What will help drive culture change is a clear vision of the future, sustained activity and a compelling story. Change needs to be brought to life for those who will be required to make the journey. Attention must always be paid to the feelings of those who are experiencing change. For some, change is concerning or even frightening. It may trigger fears about job security, control or status. For others, that same change is exciting and full of new opportunities. The needs of each group must be identified and met along the way. The lack of focus on the human factor has often been identified as a fundamental weakness in many change processes.

There has been a great deal written about leading successful organization change, and a range of different models that can be used to guide approaches and activity. One such leading model on implementing successful culture change is Kotter's model of change. Some of the recommendations in this model are discussed throughout this book, such as the need to identify and then remove barriers to change (barriers to flexible working adoption were discussed in Chapter 7).

Kotter's eight-step change model

As the name suggests, the model developed by John Kotter (2012) for leading change involves eight separate but related steps for success. Kotter's model is very detailed, so we will consider only a few of the elements here that will be specifically relevant to creating a flexible working culture shift.

The first step in this model is to create a sense of urgency about the change. This is about explaining why the change is not only necessary, but also why it is necessary *now*. The information that can support this phase of communication is detailed in Part One of this book. It is a critical part of the journey that employees understand why the change is urgent.

Another crucial step (discussed in detail in Chapters 9 and 11) is the need to create a compelling vision for the future and then communicate it well. A compelling vision is one that can be explained simply and quickly, and that is simultaneously powerful and convincing. It is the 'why' which is driving you to implement a new approach to flexibility. This may also involve the need to explain the risks to the organization of not changing. In the context of flexible working, this could include the potential for issues such as employee turnover, reduced ability to recruit talent in the future or negative impacts on employee engagement and wellbeing.

In the various steps of the model, Kotter tells us to pay particular attention to:

- Rewarding and celebrating the contributions of those who are involved in supporting the change (consider, for example, public recognition for flexible working role models and champions).

- Creating short-term/quick wins. This could include setting some goals relating to flexible working in your operational plan that you can deliver quickly, providing a boost to the implementation team but also signalling success of the project to the wider organization.

- Sharing success stories on a regular basis (this is discussed more in Chapter 11).

- Developing a process to address people's concerns or issues related to the change. For a flexible working change programme, this could be achieved through tools and guidance and identifying individuals who can provide more detailed conversations and support.

- Forming a powerful team that can guide the change initiative, involving people from across the organization, and from all levels of the hierarchy. Change does not just begin from the top; it is delivered bottom-up, too.

- Involving a range of stakeholders to input into the development of the change. We will discuss this in more depth in Chapter 9 on developing flexible working policy.

There are, of course, other ideas about implementing organizational change. Different models of change emphasize the importance of similar actions including effective communication, ongoing activity, creating a big picture vision and the psychological impacts upon individuals involved. Most research into change also notes the particular problem of change resistance. Many employees are now used to working in organizations that are constantly talking about or seeking to implement change; this can lead to the issue of 'change fatigue', where employees simply become tired of being on the receiving end of initiative after initiative. Other employees will resist change for a whole range of reasons.

How do we know if employees or managers are resisting change? Simply, there will not be any real difference in the way things have always been done. In the context of flexible working specifically, look out for these potential indicators:

- data hotspots that indicate a more than average amount of flexible working applications are being turned down, few employees are working flexibly or jobs are not advertised as suitable for flexible working;

- managers are openly complaining about the strategy or policy, or suggesting that it will not work in their team or part of the organization;

- managers are identifying issues or problems with the strategy or policy, but are not offering any potential solutions or workarounds;

- lack of willingness to undertake training on flexible working;

- employees are unwilling to use or learn how to use the technology that will enable some forms of flexible working.

Any of these indicators may suggest additional, targeted activity is required. Depending on the signs and how widespread they appear to be, this may be organization-wide action, or some specific steps in problem areas.

Another leading writer on organizational change, Kurt Lewin, cautions organizations about assuming that reaching the desired state means that the change process has been a success, as it is possible for success to be only temporary or short term, regressing quickly back to the former ways of working or previously dominant culture (Lewin, 1947). In the context of flexible working, this means we should not be complacent if initial data suggests good progress. Continual assessment of your activity and culture is essential, as is the continual reinforcement of the new strategy and approach if long-term results are to be achieved.

In Chapter 9 we will explore more about how to assess the level of readiness a culture has for change. Where change is undertaken effectively, significant benefits can be realized. The following case study gives an example of an organization that has truly managed to create a flexible working culture for its staff.

CASE STUDY
Zurich Insurance Group

Zurich Insurance Group is one of the world's largest insurance groups, with about 55,000 employees serving customers in more than 170 countries, and has been delivering insurance products for over 140 years. Its main business segments are general insurance (including property, accident, car and liability insurance), life insurance, pensions and savings and investments.

In the UK, Zurich have been focusing on flexible working for several years. One of their primary drivers for doing so was the changing world of work and the nature of families. They recognized, partly prompted by feedback from their own people, that what employees wanted from their employers was also changing.

Initially, Zurich began their flexible working journey by piloting flexible working in a variety of different areas across the organization, quickly identifying that there were both business and people benefits from doing so. Their people told them that they felt more balanced, that they were able to combine work with the things they really wanted to do in their lives, as well as meet other important family commitments. The more they piloted flexible working, the more they heard the same feedback. Engagement rose in those areas and people were reporting that they felt more productive; flexible working quickly became a differentiator in the labour market.

Eventually the decision was made to stop running pilots and embrace flexible working throughout the organization.

Now, all vacancies are advertised as available as potential part-time, job-share or full-time working opportunity. This has led to an increase in female job applicants across all levels from 32 to 40 per cent. Over the same period, senior management roles have seen a more pronounced increase in applications from females, with overall applications increasing by 45 per cent.

Existing Zurich employees also have the option to request to work on a part-time, job-share or FlexWork basis (Zurich's internal brand name for its flexible working programme). Currently, 72 per cent of employees undertake FlexWork, which sets out to empower employees to work where, when and how they choose. FlexWork is agreed on an individual-to-manager or team basis.

Zurich's aim is to make their business the most attractive place to work for the widest variety of people, and offering flexible working is part of that wider goal. There are no formal targets in respect of flexible working; instead, the organization chose to start from the assumption that flexible working would be available to anyone that wanted it.

On the practical implementation of flexible working, there have been challenges along the way; one particular challenge is how to ensure that individuals do not become isolated and teams still function well and come together regularly. It has also taken time to introduce the technology that has enabled everyone to work remotely.

Feedback from employees has been consistently positive, and they commented that the ability to work flexibly has significantly benefited their lives.

As flexible working has become embedded throughout the organization, so has people's willingness to be open about their own personal flexibility. It is not uncommon, for example, for employees to post about it on their internal social media site. Employees say it makes a real difference to them to hear and see people (especially senior leaders) talk about their own flexibility. Head of HR Steve Collinson says that this approach gives people permission: if you can see it, you can be it.

Although flexible working is available for everyone at Zurich, its flexible working policy is also aligned with an industry-leading package of family policies that includes enhanced maternity, paternity and shared parental leave, as well as additional leave provision for employees undergoing IVF treatment or who experience a miscarriage or premature birth. Collinson reflects that this is part of that same broad people goal: making Zurich the most attractive employer for the widest range of people – both existing and potential employees. The development of the policy suite came directly from engaging with employees about the benefits that mattered to them.

For Zurich, flexible working is about trust and empowerment. Flexible working works most effectively in a culture of good communication and open conversations.

They use internal communication to encourage understanding of what flexible working is, and is not. Broadly, people managers have been supportive of flexible working, something that Collinson attributes to the fact that managers are employees too, and many of them also benefit from working flexibly. They have the same challenges and commitments as the people that work for them, with the increased responsibility of managing a team.

NEXT STEPS

1 Reflect on where your organization is right now against the six elements of a flexible working culture. Identify those areas that will need the most focus in your strategy and implementation plan.

2 Consider the gaps between where you are now and where you will need to be in order to be a truly flexible organization. The resources in Chapter 9 will help you assess how to tackle these gaps.

3 Revisit the barriers discussed in Chapter 7. Identify which are most relevant to your organizational culture.

4 Identify the specific actions that will be required under the culture change plan. Give particular consideration to what resistance might be received and why.

5 Review the ideas on change management from Lewin and Kotter and consider which ones are important for your particular context – and how they might be addressed.

6 Develop your compelling vision for flexible working: how can you define what you are doing and why you are doing it in a compelling and easy to understand way, accessible for both an internal and external audience?

KEY TAKEAWAYS

- There are at least six main elements of a truly flexible working organization which can be considered as building blocks to developing flexible culture. Each of these elements needs to be considered and acted upon, in addition to the recommendations set out regarding development strategy and implementation.

- Some organizations may identify other elements that are unique to them and their own particular context.

- These building blocks are interconnected and mutually supporting. Each must be worked on in order to lead to a sustainable culture shift.

- Flexible working will not happen by accident. Its adoption (and the move towards the six elements) will need to be supported through a range of initiatives and activities.

- Changing culture means changing attitudes, beliefs and behaviours. This is not necessarily a quick process and will require consistent effort.

- A formal culture change plan may be required. Organizations should consider how change can be led and enabled through the use of an appropriate culture change model.

- A good place to begin the culture change journey is to develop a compelling vision and definition of success for your new flexible working strategy and approach.

References

Kotter, J (2012) *Leading Change*, Harvard Business Review Press, Boston, MA

Lewin, K (1947) Frontiers in group dynamics: Concept, method and reality in social science; social equilibria and social change, *Human Relations*, vol 1, Issue 1, pp 5–41

Zurich UK (2019) Press release, www.zurich.co.uk/en/about-us/media-centre/company-news/2019/what-would-happen-if-you-could-apply-for-every-job-on-a-part-time-basis (archived at https://perma.cc/HDK7-NVAT)

09

Developing a strategy for flexible working

An effective strategy will consider each of the necessary elements for a flexible working culture, as discussed in Chapter 8. A strategy may stand alone or it may be part of a people or HR strategy or exist within an organization-wide plan. Strategies are typically long term in nature; they are about the big picture and the 'why' – an overall vision for the future, at least a few years ahead. Accompanying any strategy will be an operational plan which addresses the steps that must be taken in order to support it. An effective strategy will also include detail on timescales, resources and responsibilities.

The purpose of this chapter is to identify the stages necessary for the development of clear vision and strategy for flexible working, as well as what should be included in the supporting operational plan. These stages are detailed in the form of sequential steps to follow. Combined with later chapters on policy development and communication it aims to provide a blueprint for achieving a flexible working culture.

Step One: Determining the flexible working strategy

There are a number of key considerations prior to developing a strategic approach, as well as some questions that can help to aid reflection:

- What is the organization's overall aim for introducing flexibility?
- *Why* does it want to do this?
- What does flexible working mean for the specific organization – and which forms of flexibility will be most beneficial to the particular context?
- How does flexible working align with or support wider organizational objectives?

- What business benefits does it hope to realize?
- Where is the organization today in respect of the availability, acceptance and adoption of flexible working arrangements?
- What does success look like?
- If we achieve our strategy, what will we see, feel and hear in the organization in the future?

The answers to these questions should help the organization begin to build a picture of a more flexible future that is specific to them.

Where possible, try to capture the spirit of your flexible working strategy in one or two sentences that set your intentions and ambition. Later on, this can be used within the internal communications plan, helping to disseminate this vision to employees.

Readiness assessment

For many organizations, moving to more flexible forms of working will amount to a significant shift in culture, and, as we explored in Chapter 8, culture can be a difficult thing to change. The extent to which the organization is ready for a change can be assessed, and the outcomes from this process can influence the overall approach to implementation. If the strategy sets out your overall vision for the future, the readiness assessment will summarize where you are now. The operational plan and goals should fill that gap.

Readiness can be informed by data as well as by personal observations and direct feedback (see Chapter 10 for more ideas on organizational data that can also help to inform the readiness assessment). There are many areas that contribute to readiness. Here is a list of factors to consider:

- What current attitudes to flexible working exist in the organization? Is it openly acknowledged, is it merely tolerated or is it the exception to the norm? Do people feel as if they can ask for flexible working? Do flexible workers experience any form of stigma?
- Do you have senior executive support or a senior sponsor for this work (or can you identify one)?
- Does your desired approach for flexible working align with other organizational priorities?
- Culturally, does your organization reward performance, or presence? To what extent do you currently experience presenteeism or leavism?

- What existing organizational demands or pressures may make it difficult to implement flexible working practices? Can these be overcome?
- To what extent is flexible working (and any existing policy or process) currently understood?
- To what extent is flexible working broadly accepted by managers and employees as a way of working?
- What technology do you have that enables flexible working, and to what extent is it commonly used or available for employees?
- How capable are your current people managers, especially when it comes to adapting their management style?
- What is the current level of capability and capacity within human resources to support and enable flexible working?
- If the organization received a large volume of requests for flexible working following the launch of a new strategy, what impacts might there be?
- To what extent do you understand what employees want in relation to flexible working?
- What do senior leaders believe or say about flexible working? (If you do not know the answer to this, part of the readiness assessment can include talking to them to find out.)
- What resources do you have to implement this change – and what will you need? (Consider time, budget and any requirements for specialist or external skills or knowledge.)
- To what extent does your organization understand the potential benefits of flexible working?
- What might people's fears be about allowing more flexible forms of working?
- How well is change in your organization usually accepted?
- What areas of the organization are likely to be more resistant or need more support in implementing new ways of working?
- What are the particular barriers that exist in the organization that may prevent flexible working being effective? (Chapter 7 can help with this.)
- What potential risks can you identify from making this change?

Following reflection on these questions and completion of the readiness assessment, identify any areas of particular concern or focus: use these to inform the following steps.

Step Two: Senior leaders

As discussed in Chapter 8, supporting and enabling leaders are key elements of a flexible organization. For an organization to truly embrace and reap the benefits of flexible working, the senior leadership of that organization must be fully aware of the business benefits and be in support of the shift – not just theoretically but also visibly. The role of the senior leader in driving culture change cannot be overstated.

Even when senior leaders have accepted the rationale for flexible working and approved it as a strategic approach, it will take significant time and effort, probably over a sustained period, to enable it and realize its full potential across the organization. Senior leaders are the starting point – it is where the shift begins, but not where it ends. Action will be required from the top, the middle and the bottom – but senior leaders can make or break an initiative like flexible working.

It may be that the drive towards flexibility has emerged from the senior team, so it may not be necessary to put together a business plan to gain buy-in. On the other hand, where it is being proposed *to* the senior team, such as through human resources, a strategy for gaining agreement will be necessary. Undoubtedly, leaders will want to know, when it comes to flexible working, what is in it for them: what are the benefits to the organization of changing or improving the approach to flexibility. These benefits have already been set out at length in earlier chapters; the challenge is to bring these to life in a way that speaks to individual leaders and their specific context, issues and concerns. The evidence in Part One of the book can be shared with leaders to help build a business case if this is required.

Senior leaders will need context and evidence. They will need to understand costs and risks, as well as have any concerns addressed and allayed. Consider the following:

- Developing a formal business case setting out costs, benefits, estimates and risks. Include each of the steps set out in this chapter. Include timescales, responsibilities, resources and specific deliverables, as well as actions related to each of the six elements of flexible working set out in Chapter 8.

- Proposing goals and an outline operational plan.

- Identifying the particular concerns that senior leaders may have about shifting to flexible forms of working. How can you address these with evidence?

- Providing your own relevant internal data into flexible working, as well as projections for the future (see Chapter 10 for ideas about potential sources of data).

- Including your 'asks' – what you need from them to ensure success.

If senior leaders are supportive, where possible identify a sponsor for the flexible working strategy and plan. This will help to show employees and managers that this strategy has support from the top of the organization, improving credibility and giving permission.

Of course it is not just senior leaders that need to buy into a change like this; shifting culture requires a significant number of people within the organization to be part of the journey, and this can take time. Not everyone, including senior leaders, will accept a business case, no matter how well re-searched or based in evidence. Some people will naturally prefer their own beliefs and feelings.

When any new idea or innovation comes along, it will typically be adopted over a period of time, something that is often referred to as the 'innovation diffusion (or adoption) curve'. Developed by Everett Rogers (2003), it was initially used to describe technology but can also be applied to other new ideas. This process is represented visually by a bell-shaped curve through which the innovation or idea moves over a variable period of time. The first group to accept or use a new innovation are the 'innovators'; they are the risk takers, keen to try new things. Following them are the 'early adopters', who are also quick to adopt the new innovation; they can help to influence others and shape opinions around the new innovation. Next are the 'early majority' who adopt a new idea or innovation once there is evi-dence of its benefits; they are often concerned about cost. Following the early majority are the 'late majority'; a more conservative or sceptical group who will only tend to adopt an idea when they are pressurized to do so or when the majority have already adopted it. Finally, there are the 'laggards'. This is the most conservative group of all and they are very reluctant to change. They will only adopt an idea when it is mainstream – and often when the original idea is no longer new and others have moved on to even newer ideas or thinking.

As one example of this diffusion, consider the mobile phone. Mobiles were first available in the early 1980s, although they looked very different to the devices we all typically carry today. When they were initially launched they were expensive, and were only used by a relatively small number of people – the innovators. Over time, mobile phones became steadily more popular. The early majority, the late majority and then the laggards joined in. People needed to see why they needed a phone, believe that they would be able to use it, and adopt it into everyday life. Throughout this journey mobiles also became cheaper, smaller and more reliable. More and more features were added. Now we are at a point where most people have some sort of mobile phone device, no matter how long it took them to adopt it.

Rogers' theories concerning diffusion of ideas have other relevance to the adoption of flexible working: the elements that influence the speed of adoption. These include the innovation itself, communication channels used to spread the idea, time, and the social system in which the idea is taking place. With every new idea there is a point at which critical mass is reached and the idea goes mainstream – just like the mobile phone. Flexible working is yet to reach this tipping point: we are only part-way through the adoption curve, and therefore those organizations who are embracing flexibility, some of whom are described in this book, might still be considered innovators or early adopters. Those organizations who believe that flexible working (or indeed any new idea related to the world of work) is not for them are those groups towards the end of the curve. They are the late majority or the laggards. Despite the mounting evidence that flexible working is replete with benefits and highly desired by employees, they hold onto the old ways whilst their competitors reap the rewards of earlier adoption. In later chapters we will return to this issue, and discuss ways that those individuals who are resistant to change or new ideas can be tackled in order to support the strategy.

Step Three: Goals

After the overall approach to flexible working has been determined and agreed with senior leaders, the next step will be to set some specific goals in order to achieve it. Goals (and the operational plan) should also be informed by the outcomes of the readiness assessment.

When it comes to setting goals, many readers will be familiar with the acronym SMART: specific, measurable, achievable, realistic and time-bound. This approach can be used as a framework to ensure that any goals set are appropriate and reasonable, as well as provide a standard for measuring progress and success in the future. There is one word of caution, however, when using SMART goals. The framework can be quite rigid, and may not actually support organizations with high ambition, or who genuinely want to see a revolution. Some of the greatest visions were not especially achievable or realistic at their outset (for example, the United States' aim to put a man on the moon in the 1960s may have been specific and measurable but was probably not considered very realistic or achievable!). Goals also need to be ambitious and include some stretch in order to increase motivation.

There are some ideas detailed in Step Five (getting ready for launch) that may also form one of your goals or part of the operational plan. Other potential goals or key performance indicators could include:

- awareness of your flexible working policy amongst all employees;
- managers who have undertaken training in flexible working;
- manager perceptions of flexible working;
- improved employee perceptions about flexibility in their work or working patterns;
- increased numbers of job applications;
- the number of vacancies advertised as suitable for flexible working;
- an overall target of employees working flexibly;
- internal movement of flexible workers;
- cost savings through real estate;
- reduced absenteeism;
- reduced carbon footprint from employee commuting;
- employee engagement levels;
- employee retention/turnover figures.

Once you have established your key goals, these can inform Step Four – your operational plan. Finally, consider whether, as part of your communication strategy, you want to share these goals with your employees in the interests of transparency and engagement.

Step Four: Operational planning

Your operational plan is simply the detail of what you are going to do and when you are going to do it, as well as who will be responsible for delivery. This plan will need to include subjects such as policy development and communication, which we will consider in more detail in Chapters 10 and 11. The overall plan does not need to be long or complex as long as it is clear.

In addition to those areas, there are a few other subjects that you may wish to include in your plan:

- Identifying your own particular barriers and myths operating within your organizational context and what you will do to tackle them. Refer to Chapters 6 and 7 to guide you in this reflection.

- Whether or not you need a new or revised policy for flexible working. If you believe that you do, refer to Chapter 10 to aid you in the development of this document.

- Key milestones and dates and when they will be achieved so that you can identify if the appropriate progress is being made. If it is not you can adapt your approach accordingly.

- A process for reporting back to senior leaders on progress against the strategy and specific goals.

Once your plan is finalized, you can move on to getting your new strategy or approach ready for launch.

Step Five: Getting ready for launch

Chapter 11 will provide considerable detail on the steps that may need to be taken prior to launch in order to prepare the organization and its managers, with a particular emphasis on communication. This section details some other optional ideas that you may wish to consider to support your launch of flexible working, or that may form one of your goals or part of the operational plan. These ideas are also linked to the discussion in Chapter 8 about changing organizational cultures.

Pilot schemes

The organization can decide to launch their new approach to flexible working to the entire organization at the same time or alternatively choose to undertake a pilot scheme first.

Where there is concern about the impact of flexibility on the organization, or where the organizational culture is one that is generally risk-averse, a pilot scheme can be a good way to get buy-in and persuade the sceptics. It can also help to build an evidence base specific to the organization. Although some forms of flexible working are undoubtedly taking place in almost all organizations, a pilot scheme can be used to expand them or try entirely new types of working arrangement for the organization. Examples could include some of those more infrequently used forms of flexible working discussed in Part One, such as compressed hours or nine-day fortnights. Pilot schemes can last for a time period determined by the organization, although a period of at least several months would be required to truly assess impact, costs and benefits. Pilot schemes could also extend to other aspects of flexible working such as recruitment, with a pilot to advertise certain job roles as suitable for flexible working.

A pilot scheme can initially be undertaken on a small scale, perhaps in just one team or department, and scaled up if appropriate. It will help to assess feasibility and gather useful data from which the organization can learn for the future. Such a scheme can be operated on the basis that it is a trial and there should be no expectation of continuance, as this will depend entirely on the results and outcomes. During a pilot of any new forms of flexible working, there will not be any permanent change to terms and conditions of employment for participating employees. Following the conclusion of a pilot it will be helpful to undertake both a qualitative and quantitative analysis of outcomes by looking at organizational data on productivity, absence, engagement and costs, as well as having discussions with and feedback from individual employees about their experiences of working differently during the duration of the pilot scheme.

Proactive conversations

Typically, flexible working conversations are reactive. Flexibility is discussed when an employee raises the issue, whether informally or via a formal flexible working request. Research by Timewise (2019) found that very few managers proactively discuss flexible working options with their teams; only 1 in 5 said that they had taken the initiative to discuss flexible working with their team or had proactively offered it. Only 19 per cent said that they had offered it during recruitment and selection. Where an organization truly wishes to embrace flexibility, managers can be encouraged to raise flexibility proactively with their teams, through 121s, performance appraisals or team meetings. This can send a powerful signal to employees that this is an acceptable conversation to have. How to have an effective conversation can be included in flexible working training for line managers (also discussed further in Chapter 11).

Email

Chapter 5 discussed the potential dangers to employee wellbeing of being 'always on', and the potential in our ever-connected world to have a blurring of the boundaries between work and home. Email is part of this; sending and receiving emails out of working hours or on holidays is commonplace in many organizations. A decade or so ago, before we all routinely had mobile devices containing our work emails, in the default model work stayed at the workplace. Today, as well as email being constantly available on our phones or portable tablets, there is a multitude of other ways that we are constantly contactable. Social media networks, work online chat groups and text messages are just a few of the ways that we can receive ongoing contact from colleagues or managers. For some, this can be a stressful experience and contribute to work–life balance issues.

Some people feel that there should be a ban on sending emails outside of 'office hours', and there are organizations that do take proactive steps to discourage email on weekends and evenings. Some go even further. In France the 'right to disconnect' is included in national legislation; companies with more than 50 employees are legally required to negotiate with employee representatives in order to determine the conditions of use relating to email tools. At German company Daimler employees have the choice when on holiday to use a program that automatically deletes their emails, replying to the sender that the recipient is on leave and re-directing their query (Time, 2014).

However well-intentioned some of these initiatives may be, they can present a problem for flexible working; flexible working fundamentally challenges the notion of normal 'office hours'. If we ban email (or other forms of work-based communication) after 5pm then this only serves to perpetuate the idea that normal work takes place at this time, and anything else is 'other' and reinforces the default model of work. In fact, recent research from the University of Sussex found that policies restricting email might actually harm wellbeing – the very opposite of what such policies are usually intending, as it reduced employees' control over their own work schedule (Russell and Woods, 2019). As with many of the subjects discussed in this book, there is no simple, one-size-fits-all solution.

When adopting flexible working it is inevitable that some employees will work alternative schedules, and will be working at times that their colleagues are not. It is important to set out an overall approach to this to avoid the potential for negative impacts upon wellbeing and increasing presenteeism or leavism (working whilst on holiday or other forms of leave). This is especially important for senior leaders, to whom employees will look for guidance about what is culturally acceptable. Consider creating email etiquette guides, the use of auto-signatures that explain the sender works flexibly and will not be available to receive responses immediately, or encouraging leaders to have conversations with the team about their own schedule. Alternatively, if a response is not required, employees can choose to complete their work and send emails at a later point when the recipient is more likely to be working. There are many simple tools within email software that can support this. Email culture can quickly become problematic; flexible working must not add to cultural or individual stress. This will undermine your flexible working ambitions.

Job-share matching

Job-sharing can be an underused form of flexible working. This may be because of the difficulties of finding a suitable job-share partner, as well as working out the practicalities of the sharing itself. In practice, job-shares often arise when two individuals identify an opportunity and make a case to do so. There can be real benefits to job-share arrangements when they are well designed. Organizations can get two sets of experience, skills and knowledge, and it can help to retain employees who might otherwise have left the organization – and in recruitment terms it can open up new talent pools from which to hire. One option to encourage and enable job-sharing is for the organization to take a more active role in matching individuals who are interested in this form of flexible working, and who might have complementary skills and experience. For example, consider creating a simple register of interest, or even an online space for employees to connect with colleagues for these purposes, with the option to share information about the kinds of roles for which they would be interested in exploring possible job-sharing.

Job design

Job design is defined by the CIPD (2019) as 'the process of establishing employees' roles and responsibilities and the systems and procedures that they should use or follow'.

Job design is a broad discipline, and takes into account a range of factors including quality of work, job purpose, capability, productivity and even motivation theory. In reality, many jobs are not designed at all; they evolve over time or are influenced by the employee who is undertaking the work and their particular skills and experience. Where jobs are formally designed, this is often within areas that lend themselves to automation or monitoring. It is, for example, easier to design work as it flows through a production line than for an academic undertaking research or teaching. For the purposes of this book, we are concerned with issues that relate to the design of flexible work, and reduced-hours working in particular. Care must be taken that flexible workers do not have an inappropriate workload that is not commensurate with their working hours and patterns. This can be a common issue when an employee who has previously worked full-time hours begins to undertake some form of time flexibility, particularly by reducing their hours. All too often, that employee continues to undertake a similar workload to the one they had prior to the change, and tries to fit this into a shorter working week. There are obvious implications here, especially in relation to wellbeing and the potential for work-related stress.

To avoid this occurring when an employee changes hours, the design of the job needs to be considered and amended where necessary. This may be as simple as reviewing workloads and either amending timescales or reducing overall requirements. At the other end of the spectrum, and depending on the form of flexibility to be undertaken, this may necessitate a much broader review of the overall requirements of the job role. Following the acceptance of requests or during trial periods, managers should be encouraged to review job descriptions with the flexible worker, as well as review any objectives set under internal performance management systems, and adapt them accordingly. Initially, this may involve a period of trial and error, and continued dialogue between the employee and the manager may be necessary to ensure workloads are appropriate.

Redesigning jobs following receipt or acceptance of a flexible working request is, however, only one aspect of job design considerations. Job design is also relevant at the point of recruitment. When a recruitment need arises, all too often in practice the recruitment requirement is based on what went before – either in terms of the tasks noted in the formal job description or through seeking a similar individual with similar skills and experience. In many cases, this will also mean recruiting for the same hours and working patterns. If this is the default working model, then the potential for flexibility may be overlooked. Only by reviewing the job requirements and thinking about the overall job design can a job be opened up to flexibility – as well as a new pool of talent. In the next section we will turn to the need for manager training. Managers should be encouraged (and supported) to re-view job descriptions and focus on the results and outcomes required of a given job role, rather than tasks and hours worked.

The key to job design is proactivity – not waiting for an employee to raise a workload issue but taking active steps to ensure that workload and objectives are aligned appropriately to the working pattern undertaken by the individual. Good job design will be a two-way process, involving constructive dialogue between employee and manager, taking into account the needs and responsibilities of both parties.

Technology

As we have already discussed in Chapter 3, technology is a key trend in the future of work. It is an enabler of flexible working, allowing individuals to work remotely and teams to connect and collaborate asynchronously (at different times). We have also identified that a lack of available technology, or indeed a lack of ability or willingness to use it, is a barrier to effective flexible working. Almost all of the technology that any individual or team will need to enable flexible working is readily available on most corporate networks or is inexpensive (if not free) to use. A wifi connection is the most fundamental requirement for flexible working, along with a laptop and some form of virtual access to corporate networks or shared spaces.

However, the availability of technology does not mean that it will be easily or readily adopted. As we have already discussed, new technology takes some time to diffuse through an organization. The technology adoption model (Davis, 1989) tells us that the take-up of technology is typically influenced by two main factors: its perceived usefulness and its perceived ease of use. The first relates to the extent an individual believes that using a particular piece of technology at work will be useful to them; for example, it may help them to enhance their performance. The second is related to the individual's belief that the technology will be easy for them to use. If it is not, they may simply not bother. Remember, even if a particular piece of technology seems easy or intuitive, not everyone will feel the same and may require support.

The technology challenge in relation to flexible working is complicated by a further issue – it is not just the flexible worker that needs to adopt it, but potentially their colleagues and managers too in order to facilitate effective communication where employees are not in the location or working at the same times. If the colleague or manager sees no benefit to themselves in using a particular technology, one of the two main influencing factors in adoption of the technology falls, even if the second can be met.

Technology in the workplace is everywhere and it has the potential to reshape much of how we work. Not everyone, however, is comfortable in using it. Consider the following:

- What technology will work best for your organization's flexible workers? Is this currently available on your corporate network?

- Will there be any costs associated with additional technology, and how will these be met?

- How will you ensure that this technology is available, supported and used?

- What training will be required to help people use it – and who will deliver this?

- What barriers exist to technology use in your particular organization?

Finally, communication is a critical step within the operational plan, and will also need to form part of Step Five – getting ready for launch. It is absolutely essential that the overall strategy for flexible working is fully communicated, including those specific goals and targets set by the organization. This can be accompanied with a clear 'why' statement: why the organization has chosen to take this approach and what it believes will be the benefits to all parties. Achieving effective communication will be considered in depth in Chapter 11.

NEXT STEPS

1 Answer the questions set out in Step One in order to determine the desired approach to flexibility for your organization.

2 Undertake a readiness assessment to identify how prepared or ready the organization is to move towards flexible working, and how likely it is to be accepted or embraced. Engage with senior leaders in this work. Use the outcomes from this assessment to inform your operational plan.

3 Reflect on the innovation adoption curve. Where do you feel your organization typically fits into this structure? Are you normally innovators or laggards? Use this idea to help you with your operational plans.

4   Identify a senior leader who is willing to act as active and visible sponsor for your flexible working initiatives.

5   Set some specific goals or key performance indicators (KPIs) that align to the agreed strategic approach in order that success and progress can be measured. To ensure your plan is manageable, consider beginning with just three or four key goals.

6   Consider the ideas set out in Step Five. Are any of them suitable for your strategy or organizational context?

7   Write your operational plan to underpin your strategy and goals. Get this and the previous step formally approved where necessary.

8   Refer to Step Five, and decide if you want to undertake any of these supporting activities. If so, add them to your operational plan.

9   Engage with your IT team on the issue of technology. Discuss how you can work together to ensure flexible workers and their colleagues have what they need to be entirely effective.

10   As part of the operational plan, refer back to the chapters on myths (Chapter 6) and barriers (Chapter 7). Identify which are the particular areas that need to be tackled for the particular organizational context.

KEY TAKEAWAYS

- The organization will need to determine an overall strategy for flexible working, accompanied by practical and achievable goals.

- Initially, set a small number of goals for flexible working, against which you can measure success. Keep these under review and revise them when necessary.

- Senior leaders are key to success. The flexible working strategy will need to be approved and endorsed, and wherever possible have a senior level sponsor or advocate.

- Every organization will have its own level of readiness in relation to moving towards flexible working. This will influence the goals, operational plan and implementation approach.

- The strategy and goals will need to be translated into an operational plan. The plan will include the various steps that will be taken in order to achieve the strategy and goals.

- There is a range of complementary steps or initiatives that can aid the strategy and form part of the plan. Examples include job-share matching programmes, pilot schemes and technology.

- Jobs may need to be redesigned to ensure that employees who work flexibly (particularly reduced-hours workers) are not overloaded.

References

CIPD (2019) *Job Design Factsheet*, www.cipd.co.uk/knowledge/strategy/organizational-development/job-design-factsheet (archived at https://perma.cc/63U9-ZSYR)

Davis, FD (1989) Perceived usefulness, perceived ease of use, and user acceptance of information technology, *MIS Quarterly*, **13** (3)

Rogers, E (2003) *Diffusion of Innovations*, 5th edn, Free Press

Russell, E and Woods, S (2019) Personality differences as predictors of action-goal relationships in work email activity, *Computers in Human Behaviour*, vol 103, pp 67–79

Time (2014) *Here's a Radical Way to End Vacation Email Overload*, time.com/3116424/daimler-vacation-email-out-of-office/ (archived at https://perma.cc/P7SD-Y4LL)

Timewise (2019) *Proactive Approaches to Discussing Flexible Working*, timewise.co.uk/article/proactive-approaches-flexible-working/ (archived at https://perma.cc/SLF4-6ZC2)

10

Effective policy and process

An effective and well-used policy is one of the six elements of a flexible workplace. In an organization where flexible working has been truly accepted it is theoretically possible to reduce the reliance on policy and formal processes, with managers and employees empowered to work a multitude of flexible ways. There are plenty of examples of organizations that have done just this, but the culture of the organization concerned needs to be ready to support such an approach. For many organizations this is some way into the future. Where flexible working is not broadly accepted, particularly by people managers, a lack of policy and process could leave individual employees vulnerable to the personal attitudes and beliefs of unsupportive or 'command and control' style management. On the basis that a formal, documented policy and process will almost always be required, this chapter sets out a range of good practice recommendations and further considerations for successful policy approaches.

The policy and procedure published by an organization is influential in a number of ways, both on the actions of individual employees as well as the overall culture. It can support broader organizational change, provide a clear statement of intent and define parameters. The language used in the written document can help to set the tone for flexible working; it can either be encouraging, welcoming and friendly, or bureaucratic, complex and off-putting – and unfortunately there are many examples of the latter to be found in HR departments everywhere. The formal process that is set out for employees to follow when making an application is also important. Ideally, processes should be easy to follow, as brief as possible and no more formal than absolutely necessary. Policy and process alike should work together to facilitate a meaningful conversation between the parties – the primary focus should not be on following the process itself but effective dialogue. However, a policy on its own will not transform a culture or make a shift in attitudes. It is merely one consideration in the flexible working journey.

To ensure that the policy supports culture change and enables true flexibility there are a number of recommendations to consider, as this chapter will explore. Above all, a flexible working policy must be tailored to the organization for which it applies. It is not about replicating best practice developed at other places, but designing best fit for each organization. All too often policies and procedures are based on standard templates or 'borrowed' from other organizations. This approach might tick all the necessary legal boxes, but may well lead to a sub-optimal document that will not meet the unique needs of the individual workplace. Flexible working is, of course, contextual.

It is important to remember that the legislation, as set out in Chapter 1, sets a *minimum* standard of rights in relation to requesting flexible working arrangements. It is therefore a starting point; the policy does not (and indeed should not if flexibility is to be truly enabled) simply state the law or the accompanying code of practice.

Preparation for policy development

Before commencing any review of existing policy or process or design of a new policy, it is good practice to first undertake a review of existing organizational data. This will help you understand more about your current picture of flexibility. Consider reviewing some or all of the following:

- Who works flexibly in the organization now? When, how and where are they working?
- What are the specific forms of flexible working being undertaken – and which are not in use?
- What proportion of current employees have some form of time or location flexibility?
- How many requests are received on average, monthly or annually? Who is making them?
- Is the overall request trend up, down or stable – and what might be the cause of any changes?
- How many requests are accepted and how many are rejected? In the case of the latter, what are the reasons for those rejections, and who is responsible for them?

- Who gets promoted now? Did they work flexibly before their promotion – or afterwards?

Review the data, both in whole and split by sex, in order to identify important differences between male and female staff. Data needs to be first reviewed at an organization level and then at a departmental one to identify any problematic trends specific to some teams or functions. This data will help to identify areas that the policy and process need to address – as well as what myths may be present within the organization that can be tackled through communication and awareness raising. We will discuss this element more in later chapters.

Before putting pen to paper the second step in effective policy development is to ensure appropriate input from a variety of internal groups. HR policy is too often designed solely by HR teams without input from stakeholders, other than perhaps where there is a recognized trade union with which to consult. The development of a flexible working policy (and any accompanying guidance and training) can benefit from the input of employees who work flexibly or who have experienced the application process, successfully or otherwise. During the design of new or the review of existing policy, engage with employees and seek useful information. One key area for exploration is the current employee experience of flexible working by looking into aspects including:

- What reactions have employees noticed from managers and colleagues?
- How quickly and effectively was their flexible working request dealt with?
- What barriers have they faced when working flexibly, whether practical or attitudinal?
- How easy was any existing policy and process to understand and follow?

Also, talk to those employees who had their requests for flexibility rejected to understand why and how this was communicated – what was *their* experience of the existing processes? Finally and perhaps most importantly, how did undergoing the formal process make people *feel*? This is ultimately the very essence of employee engagement. Similar questions can be put to people managers:

- What is their experience of managing flexible working requests?
- What support do they have and what more do they feel they need?

- How confident do they feel in applying the statutory framework and any existing policy, and how well do they understand it?
- What concerns do they have about managing flexible working arrangements?

Where the organization recognizes a trade union or has a formal works council or staff committee, be sure to consult with them on the policy. As well as providing other viewpoints this will help employees to see the policy as one which has been fairly developed.

Policy: Decision-making

Once all the relevant data has been collated decisions can be made about the overall policy approach. Here are a few further recommendations for consideration.

A supporting statement

A policy will benefit from a strong opening statement that highlights the organization's support for flexible working, states that flexible working requests will be approached positively with the aim of achieving a mutually acceptable outcome, and gives a commitment to provide appropriate resources and support for flexible workers, their teams and their managers.

Day One requests

There is little benefit for the organization, manager or employee to postpone a conversation about flexible working to the 26th week of employment, as provided for under the statutory process. This can be a barrier to job applications and talent acquisition, may cause unnecessary stress to employees, and merely postpones what is likely to be an inevitable discussion. All parties would be better served by having that dialogue at an early stage – ideally at the point of recruitment or offer. If flexible working is not feasible, an organization will not waste the considerable costs associated with recruitment and training should an employee leave if they are unable to access flexibility at a later point.

Time frames

The legislation regarding flexible working provides for requests to be dealt with within three months, including an appeal where applicable. This is an unnecessarily long period and likely to cause stress to employees awaiting an important decision about their working future. It should be possible in almost all cases to deal with requests much more quickly. Setting shorter timescales for both an initial conversation and final decision will focus minds to action. Where policy and process is well drafted and accompanied with good guidance, communication and training, considering applications does not need to be an onerous or lengthy process.

Application forms

Provide employees with a simple and easy to understand form for the purposes of making their request. There is no need to ask employees why they are making a request – they should simply be required to set out the pattern that they are seeking, when they would like any new arrangements to begin, and be encouraged to think through the implications of their request and how any challenges can be overcome. Asking for reasons invites value judgements or unconscious bias, and serves no material purpose.

Addressing misuse and misconduct

It is inevitable that some employees will misuse flexible working when it is available. This is not about flexible working itself, but a fact of organizational life in the same way that a small minority of employees will spend too much time on Facebook, ring in sick when they are not genuinely ill or overclaim their expenses. There is no evidence to suggest that employees are likely to misuse flexible working arrangements any more than they are any other benefit or opportunity, but provision needs to be made to address this should it occur. Providing managers with clear guidance about how to approach such situations should they arise will make this task somewhat easier.

Human resources involvement

The myths associated with flexible working, along with potential negative attitudes which are detailed here in this book, mean that it is a very real possibility that employees asking for flexible working could be denied the opportunity to do so based on the views, attitudes and assumptions of their manager as opposed to evidence-based decision-making. HR has a role to play in ensuring this does not happen. Where it is considered this is a possible risk for an organization (or specific areas within it), it may be pertinent to provide in the policy for HR to attend relevant meetings, particularly appeals, to provide oversight into how requests are handled and responded to.

Discretion relating to requests

The statutory framework allows employees to make one flexible working request in a rolling 12-month period. This can present a challenge to some employees, as it is entirely feasible that life circumstances can change dramatically over the course of a year. A good practice approach will allow employees to bring an additional request where the manager feels that there is good reason for them to do so. Forcing employees to wait until an arbitrary time period has elapsed will not benefit either party and only delay an inevitable conversation.

Assessment criteria

It can be helpful to set out a range of criteria that the organization will take into account when considering a request. A sample tool for managers to use (Tool 1.1) is included in Appendix 1 of this book. This section of the policy does not need to be long or overly complex but should summarize the key criteria upon which managers will reach a decision, such as cost implications, impact on team, customers or operational delivery, ability to recruit (for example, in a job-share situation), potential for workload reallocation and organizational performance. A further option, taking the policy one step further, is to set out what will *not* be taken into account when reaching a decision. This could include the individual's reasons for requesting flexible working, precedent setting or the perceptions of others.

Promotion and internal vacancies

People who work flexibly, particularly part-time workers, can find themselves 'stuck' in their roles if opportunities for progression or promotion are advertised as default full-time. A policy provision that provides for automatic consideration of existing flexible working arrangements for successful internal job applicants can ensure that flexible working does not carry with it a career stigma (or become a retention risk), and encourage applications from internal candidates. An assessment of the role for flexible potential can be carried out in the same way as already set out in guidance and policy.

Appeals

There is no statutory right for employers to provide an appeal stage in the event that a flexible working request is rejected. However, whilst an appeal will undoubtedly increase the length of the process it is good practice to include one in a flexible working policy. Where there is no opportunity for an appeal, there is no oversight. If requests are being rejected unfairly or on the whim of an individual manager, this will have the potential to expose an organization to claims on an individual basis, damage employee engagement and undermine any organization-wide aims of enabling flexibility. The potential for decisions to be reviewed by more senior levels of management will go some way to mitigate the potential for bias arising from poor management behaviour.

Trial periods

Providing for (and indeed encouraging) trial periods is a policy essential. Trial periods can offer a valuable opportunity for both managers and employees to assess the benefits and challenges of a potential flexible working arrangement. They are particularly useful when the request is for a working pattern not previously undertaken. A trial period can be of any length agreed by the individuals. One to three months is typical, although it is perfectly acceptable to agree a longer trial period where more time is needed to truly assess the impact of the working arrangement. A trial period does not permanently change the terms and conditions of employment and is therefore not binding on either party for its duration. During the trial period there should be regular dialogue between the manager and employee about how the trial is proceeding, and the manager should keep notes throughout. At the end of a trial period a formal assessment should be carried out. Where the trial has been successful the organization may agree the new working pattern at which point it will have contractual effect. Where the trial period has not been successful these reasons should be fully discussed with the employee – the employee will then normally revert to their previous working arrangements or an alternative can be agreed, either for a further trial or contractually.

Localized rules

In large or complex organizations it can be difficult to create a policy that works for each part of it. One option to address this challenge is to set broad policy principles at an organizational level and then allow local teams and departments to figure out what works best for them operationally – with appropriate guidance and support. Care must be taken that some teams or departments do not develop their own policies and procedures or deviate from the broader organizational principles; this can be achieved through the provision of appropriate support and HR oversight. Consider, for example, how a team might agree some of the following:

- how they will let each other know when and where they are working (especially helpful for teams who undertake some aspects of their work remotely), such as the use of shared calendars;
- the best ways to keep in touch and update each other on activities or tasks;
- how often and when to schedule meetings that everyone can attend (for example, some teams agree to schedule office meetings between the hours of 10am–4pm, to ensure that flexi-time or staggered-hours staff can all attend);
- how flexi-time or staggered-hours schemes will operate in practice to ensure appropriate levels of office cover;
- what technology to use for updates and communications (and if any training is required to help people to use it);
- arrangements for shared office spaces.

Such an approach will increase the sense of autonomy and ownership for new ways of working for both employees and their managers.

Family policies

Whilst this book has sought to make a convincing case that flexible working is for all employees and is not (or should not be) limited to working parents, there is no doubt that flexible working is of interest and potential benefit to this particular group. As we discussed in Chapter 4 on flexible working and inclusion, there is a particularly complex picture around gender norms and the availability and implication of flexible working arrangements. If flexible working is to be truly enabled, it needs to be complemented by other policies and initiatives, some of which relate specifically to working parents, but will also complement broader challenges to gender roles and flexibility stigma.

Flexible working is a policy that cannot stand alone, and can particularly benefit from being positioned as part of a range of wellbeing and family support policies. In particular, where flexible working policies are complemented by policies that provide for enhanced paternity leave, studies have shown that fathers' involvement in childcare and domestic work will increase not only during their period of leave but for many years into the future (Nepomnyaschy and Waldfogel, 2007).This can help to change some of the problematic gender norms that relate to flexible working and reduce the stigma on flexibly working mothers.

Policies about family leave also provide an opportunity to raise awareness of flexible working. When employees are taking maternity, adoption, shared parental or other forms of leave, employers will typically need to send written communications and managers will need to hold meetings with the individual. Employers who wish to encourage or normalize flexible working can use these opportunities to include information about flexible working policies or application processes at an early stage (such as prior to maternity leave commencing). As we saw in Chapter 4, fathers can experience their own challenges and cultural barriers in terms of accessing flexible working – communicating with them via other policies (such as paternity leave) can also help to encourage applications and demonstrate that the organization is positive about flexibility.

Supporting guidance

Having an effective, well-designed and evidence-based policy is, however, not enough, even if all of the recommendations set out here are embraced. Both people managers and employees will also need practical guidance to support effective implementation and day-to-day practice. This is particularly important when flexible working is a significant shift for an organization's culture.

Employee guidance should include what is expected of them for the working pattern they are undertaking. If the agreed flexible working arrangement includes an element of home- or remote working, this should include information about how they are expected to keep in touch or be available for contact with colleagues, reporting sickness whilst working from home, safety and security of work-related property, and data and rules relating to reimbursement of expenses. Employees should also be guided to check with their mortgage provider, landlord or insurance company for any implications of necessary permissions relating to working at home. Generally, most organizations will insist that employees are not undertaking caring responsibilities at the same time as working – in particular, parents should not be caring for children whilst working their contractual hours. Employees may also need practical support with maintaining a good work–life balance when working from home, as discussed in Chapter 5 – with this form of flexible working there is potential for 'overspill' of work into non-work life and activities. This can be aligned with or built into other workplace wellbeing initiatives around supporting positive work–life balance.

In most organizations, it is the immediate line manager who is responsible for handling flexible working requests, including making the decision on whether or not a request is accepted. Managers will therefore need additional, practical information and guidance in order to ensure effective and consistent policy application – and good decision-making. A lack of consistency will inevitably lead to perceptions of unfairness and negative impacts on working relationships. Human resources can provide valuable support (and indeed challenge) to this part of the process.

Guidance for people managers should include the following:

- An overview of the policy and process requirements, as well as their specific responsibilities in relation to the management of applications.
- Information on how to manage conversations about flexible working during recruitment.
- Guidance on managing a trial period.
- A tool to help managers to assess a job for flexibility potential.
- Practical issues that arise from some forms of flexibility, such as how to calculate holiday entitlement or security requirements for homeworkers.
- Information on scaling workloads and objectives appropriately for revised working patterns. This is important to ensure that flexible workers

(particularly part-time workers) are not required to maintain the same level of output as a full-time colleague or left with a disproportionately large workload.

- A simple 'frequently asked questions' (FAQ) document that addresses those questions most asked about flexible working. This can be a good place to address some of the myths surrounding flexible working discussed previously. In particular, it is possible to address here concerns about setting precedent, suitability and managing concerns about policy misuse.

This practical guidance should be available on demand at the point of need, and be simple to understand and action. Guidance does not have to be another lengthy document for managers and employees to read. Guidance can include podcasts, flowcharts, video and simple one-page 'how to' guides and it can be complemented with real-life success stories from flexible workers within the organization. One of the most important pieces of supporting documentation is a straightforward tool to support managers in identifying whether a role has potential for flexible working. A sample guide that can be amended to suit organizational purposes and provided to people managers is included in the Flexible Working Toolkit in Appendix 1, along with other sample guides.

This information provision will help a manager to understand their responsibilities and how to fulfil them. In order, however, to support a broader cultural change towards flexible working and its acceptance across an organization, managers will need something else: the bigger picture about flexible working and why it is a business issue not an individual employee benefit. This can be combined with training on adapting their day-to-day management skills to manage flexible workers. We will explore this further in Chapter 11.

Remember, that even with an effective policy and process applied consistently, it does not necessarily follow that employees will prevail themselves of it. Where organizational culture does not effectively support flexible working, employees may not feel that they can make a request without negative career impacts or stigma. A policy document, no matter how well written, will then gather dust, unused and with benefits unrealized.

NEXT STEPS

After reading this chapter, undertake a review of your current flexible working policy and associated processes.

1 Review your current policy against the good practice recommendations set out above and identify gaps and areas for improvement.

2 Check what guidance you currently offer and identify where more support is needed or can be provided. You can use the Flexible Working Toolkit at the end of this book to help you develop your guidance documents.

3 Source relevant data on your current flexible workers and flexible working requests, and review this to identify key patterns or issues.

4 Seek feedback from flexible workers and employees who have experienced your internal processes and use this to inform your decisions relating to training, policy and communication.

5 Seek feedback from managers at various levels in the organization on their experiences of flexible working, to better inform how they can be supported as you move towards a more flexible culture.

6 Undertake a review of your family policies, including maternity, adoption, paternity and shared parental leave. As a suite, does each of these policies provide appropriate support for working parents, cross-promote flexible working, and do they link to your broader organizational goals? Too often HR policies are written with legislation or process in mind and are not designed to reflect or further broader aims and objectives.

7 Identify any other policies relevant to flexible working. For example, do you have policies or procedures relating to retirement, the menopause, equality and diversity, recruitment, sustainable travel, wellbeing or carers? Cross-reference these against your flexible working policies to ensure effective alignment and that each are mutually supporting. Ensure flexible working is referenced and signposted within each of them. Consider whether it is appropriate or necessary to introduce policies for these topics.

8 Put your policy on your external website. Be clear and transparent about your flexible offering.

KEY TAKEAWAYS

- The tone of your policy, its accessibility, the level of formality and the extent to which it is communicated and supported all send a signal to the organization about your attitudes towards flexible working.

- Policies will need to be accompanied by easy to understand guidance on how to implement it. The policy alone is not enough.

- Both managers and employees will need guidance on successful flexible working.

- Policies do not have to simply mirror the legislation – the law on flexible working should be regarded as a minimum standard. Effective flexible working will be realized when policies go above and beyond compliance.

- Flexible working policies need to align with other people policies, including those relating to family leave, carers, annual leave and codes of conduct.

- Prior to drafting policies, organizations can benefit from undertaking some research into their employees' and managers' experiences of making flexible working requests or applying current policy.

- Policy can also be supplemented with local team or department guidance on how flexible working works for them – although care should be taken that these do not deviate or undermine the organization-wide approach.

- Policies should be kept under regular review to ensure that they are supporting the organization's overall objectives relating to flexibility. Ensure they are reviewed periodically, taking into account information from your internal flexible working data.

Reference

Nepomnyaschy, L and Waldfogel, J (2007) Paternity leave and fathers' involvement with their young children, *Community, Work and Family Journal*, vol 10, pp 427–53, www.tandfonline.com/doi/abs/10.1080/13668800701575077 (archived at https://perma.cc/EC95-V8K6)

11

Supporting implementation

Following the design of the overall flexible working strategy, identification of goals and development of policy, this chapter will follow on from the steps identified in Chapter 9 and consider the supporting actions an organization will need to take to ensure effective implementation. Each of the areas discussed in this chapter should form part of the operational plan, which when enacted will support the six elements of a truly flexible workplace. The chapter will also consider communication, awareness raising, engaging other employees, and measuring progress and success. The issue of policy development, however, is so significant that it has a dedicated chapter; information on the development of policy and associated processes and guidance is contained within Chapter 10.

Communication

The first step discussed in Chapter 9 was the development of an agreed strategy and overall approach. Once this has been determined, the next and critical steps are communicating and promoting it, including helping people (managers and employees alike) with implementation.

There will need to be initial communication (especially if there is an overall or significant change in approach or policy) followed by promotion and awareness-raising activity on an ongoing basis. The continuous communication of benefits in particular will help to embed the policy and work towards ending flexibility stigma and the negative perceptions of flexible workers. There are several activities to consider at this stage of the process, each of which will complement the other. There is no one single best approach to communicating and encouraging flexible working; it will need an ongoing and concerted effort across multiple communication channels, tailored towards the specific organizational context.

Communication: The basics

The best place to begin communication is with the simple and quick steps. Ensure that flexible working, and the organization's chosen approach to it, is referenced:

- in your employee handbook if you have one;
- in any induction material or programmes for new starters;
- on your employee intranet;
- on your external website (particularly your recruitment pages);
- in management development training courses;
- in your job advertisement templates – provide a standard paragraph or simple sentence about your approach (an example is provided as Tool 1.6 in the Appendix);
- via any internal wellbeing material or programmes;
- in other relevant HR policies, including maternity leave, adoption leave, shared parental leave or carers leave, as well as standard communications to employees using these policies (such as letters confirming leave dates or employee guidance documents).

Once these areas have been addressed, it will be possible to turn to more focused activity. Here are some ideas that you may wish to consider including in your communication plan.

Explaining the benefits

Effective communication needs to include not only the details of the policy and associated processes, but the wider benefits of flexible working and its strategic relevance to the organization, especially where flexible working aligns to other organizational goals. Widespread dissemination of the business case is seen as critical for the introduction of flexible working policies (Lyonette and Baldauf, 2019).

Where the business case talks to issues of inclusion, wellbeing, sustainability and talent, flexible working is reframed and stigma reduced. It is therefore essential that throughout your communications, flexible working is clearly promoted as something that is potentially for everyone in the organization – as well as the reasons why.

By setting flexibility in the wider context of the future of work, talent acquisition, sustainability and wellbeing, flexible working can be reframed as an idea that is for and supports business – not just employees. Wherever possible, ensure that these communications are clearly supported by senior leaders. Examples could include issuing launch communications from them, including a video from senior leaders in any launch of training events, explaining why the organization is supportive of flexibility or having them attend any relevant events. Chapters 2, 4 and 5 should help you with the relevant information in order to communicate the benefits, and you can focus on the ones most relevant to your own particular organization and its goals. These benefits may be included in your launch plan, which is discussed next.

Launch

An effective launch of a new or revised approach is critical to success; it is a good news story for the organization and its people and the communication should reflect this.

There are many ways that you can launch your new approach. Consider including some of the following:

- A formal communication from a senior leader explaining the new strategy or policy, clearly outlining why the organization has decided to take this approach, and including the benefits as discussed above. This may need to be repeated across each of your company communication channels to ensure that it reaches all employees.

- A launch event. Depending on your resources and the profile you wish to give to the new strategy or approach, consider holding a dedicated event. This can be used to articulate to the organization the overall approach and its expected benefits. Wherever possible, this event should be led or attended by senior leaders to clearly demonstrate organizational commitment.

- Creating an online space where employees and managers can access your guidance, policy and toolkits, such as those included in the Flexible Working Toolkit in the Appendix.

- Establishing a way for people to ask follow-up questions for more information or to discuss personal situations or implications.

- An internal brand, name or logo for your flexible approach. You can simply choose to refer to your strategy or policy as 'flexible working'. However, having an internal brand name can help to increase its visibility, recognizability and improve engagement. An example of the use of an internal brand name is demonstrated by the case study in Chapter 8.

However you decide to communicate during the launch phase, remember that you will also need to repeat communications regularly in order to maintain awareness throughout the organization.

Managing expectations

There is one other area in relation to communication that is important when it comes to creating a positive employee experience relating to flexible working requests: the effective management of expectations. Even within an organization that is open to flexible working and has taken many steps to enable it, there will undoubtedly be requests for flexible working that cannot be accommodated. This is especially true of complex organizations with many role types; it will not be possible to create consistency of outcome even when there is consistency of process and policy application. There are many reasons why this might be the case: it may be because the hours that individuals wish to work are not possible operationally; because it is not possible to recruit (such as in relation to a job-share request); or the impact on customers or service users will be too great. Whilst this may be acceptable from a legal point of view (as they potentially amount to statutory reasons for turning down an application), rejecting requests may have an impact on morale and engagement, and perhaps more simply cause inherent feelings of unfairness.

Rather than waiting for requests to come in and then dealing with them on a case-by-case basis, organizations can take a proactive stance. Firstly, a policy can set out not just the statutory reasons that might be relied upon when considering a request, but the wider considerations that will be taken into account, relevant to the organizational context. It is also entirely possible to include, possibly in guidance notes or information on employee intranet sites, what it may or may not typically be able to accommodate. For example, a school could state that, although it will consider all requests fairly and reasonably on their own merits, it will often be unable to accommodate teachers who want to work 10 to 2, flexi-time or homeworking as this would not be when classes need to be staffed, but that they will aim to support job-shares wherever possible. Similarly, schools could also state that they would consider term-time only working for all administrative staff. Statements such of these can go some way to both avoiding requests that are unlikely to be accepted, therefore avoiding disappointment as well as encouraging staff to make a more appropriate application. Remember that even with such a statement any flexible working request received must still be heard and responded to; the point of this communication is to assist employees and avoid disappointment, not to circumvent the legal process.

Engaging traditionalists and sceptics

In Chapter 7 we explored the potential barriers to flexible working and two groups were identified as being particularly resistant to flexible working arrangements (and perhaps change in general). These are the traditionalists and the sceptics (RSA, 2013). These groups may also believe some or indeed most of the myths set out in Chapter 6. Any plan for introducing flexible working can be undermined by this group, especially when they are in management positions with responsibility for considering flexible working requests. As such it may be useful to consider a specific approach to working and communicating with these individuals.

Traditionalists and sceptics can exist anywhere in an organization, but given the extent to which long-established teams will influence one another as well as mirror the beliefs and attitudes of their leader, such beliefs may well arise throughout whole teams or departments. Your data may help you to identify these groups; they will be the teams that do not have any flexible workers or agree to only its most basic forms such as part-time working. They may routinely reject requests for flexible working, or simply have no requests at all as there is a strong 'do not ask' culture. HR professionals will often have insight too, into exactly where these attitudes arise. Over time, these groups can be influenced by a change in strategic direction, but they may equally adopt an 'it does not work in our area' mentality and ignore organization-wide communications or directives. This is a particular challenge, and even though the evidence case is compelling, it is not easy to change mindsets with data. Options to tackle this group include the following:

- Provide data. Alone, data is unlikely to shift opinions and beliefs, but using the evidence base for flexible working (combined with some of the other ideas suggested here) can be part of the plan for tackling this group.

- What's in it for them? The benefits to flexibility are wide and diverse, and there is a reasonable chance that at least one of them will resonate with that particular group or individual. For example, are they finding it difficult to recruit the right people? Do they need to save costs? Do they have wellbeing issues within their team leading to high absence from work? Are their employees lacking in engagement? Do they have high staff turnover? Identify a particular issue that is of concern to them and work with them to frame flexible working as a potential solution.

- Reduce the fear factor. For some, change generates fear. Fear of something new and perhaps not understood, as well as fear of any potential implications for them or their team. Consider what might be their greatest concern. For example, is it that they will not be able to manage the team and this will then reflect on them? Could it be that they are concerned about using technology to communicate with flexible workers or that they will receive too many requests to cope with? Aim to proactively address these fears through your communication and manager training.

- Share stories from other organizations. The benefit of sharing internal success stories was discussed earlier, but it can also be helpful to share success stories from other organizations, especially those that have experienced similar challenges. Showing how others have benefited from flexible approaches, as well as how they have made it work for them, can help sceptics and traditionalists see how it can work for them too. If necessary, facilitate conversations with others, internal and external, to support this approach.

- Engage with your IT team to discuss technology for enabling flexible working; assess if any additional technology is required, whether there will be any implications of additional flexible (particularly remote) workers, and discuss options for training people (including non-flexible workers) in relevant technology.

Now we will turn to some other ideas that can help sustain momentum and aid the overall approach to communication and awareness, both at the initial launch stage and then on an ongoing basis.

Promotion

Once the initial communications have taken place it will be necessary to turn to ongoing promotion activities. There are a number of ways to promote your flexible strategy; here are some ideas that you can try.

Flexible working champions

If flexible working is to be successfully implemented, it cannot hide away or be merely tolerated; it needs to be championed and celebrated. A network of 'flexible working champions' can play a key role in raising awareness and opening up conversations about flexibility, as well as acting as successful myth-busters and role models. In some organizations, employees may be more comfortable approaching a champion for information than a human resources representative.

Flexible working champions can be anyone in the organization, although where possible they should have either experience of working flexibly themselves or managing flexible workers. In order to be effective, they will need training and support. Training should address those areas set out above for people managers, and will ideally include an overview of the relevant legislation, the internal policy and process and available guidance. They need to be equipped to answer typical questions, be aware of potential barriers and how they can be overcome, and be able to share tips for making flexible working successful.

Find your advocates and leverage their enthusiasm. Provide champions with an opportunity to get together regularly so that they can share experiences and ideas. When reviewing your flexible working approach in the future, champions can also provide a useful source of information into attitudes and beliefs. Aim to have at least one champion per department, and make their names known to employees (for example, include them on your staff intranet if you have one) so that they can be approached directly for information support.

Flexible working networking group

One way to continue the conversation about flexibility is to create an internal network for flexible workers. The purpose of such a network is to give employees a space in which they can discuss flexible working, share ideas about how to make it work for them, but also discuss challenges and barriers and support each other to overcome them. Such a network can also be linked to, or even organized by, the flexible working champion team.

Many organizations already have a range of staff networks, and they typically do not need significant resources or efforts to set them up and keep them going. Ideally a group should have a space in which they can meet that is relatively private, a small budget for refreshments and some support with internal communications. In order to generate interest and attendance the group could from time to time invite speakers or internal guests to join them and talk about relevant topics (a senior leader would be especially beneficial). Once established the group can be largely self-organizing. Ideally this would not be a group run by the organization or even HR, but by and for the benefit of its members.

Sharing success stories

Most organizations will have some employees who are currently working flexibly – although depending on the culture of that particular organization they may or may not be easy to find. Where possible, share the stories of those successfully making flexibility work for them. Consider asking them the following:

- How, when and where do they work?
- What particular forms of flexible working are they undertaking?
- How do they make it effective?
- What does it mean to them and what tips for success can they share with others?
- What barriers have they experienced and how have they overcome them?

Use these stories to bring flexible working to life for the rest of the workforce. There are many ways that you can share personal accounts: create a dedicated area on your staff intranet, develop a simple booklet (physical or virtual) or have an event that people can attend to listen to talks. To make this aspect of your communication plan meaningful, wherever possible include people from a variety of different roles and throughout the organizational hierarchy. Ideally, include stories from senior managers or leaders too. This will help to normalize flexible working at all levels of the organization, as well as help to rebut some of the myths of flexible working discussed in Chapter 6. If possible, have some success stories ready for launch, and add to them on an ongoing basis.

Manager training

According to the CIPD, providing training to people managers on the benefits of flexible working as well as how to manage flexible workers is the most effective way of increasing both the quality and quantity of flexible working arrangements (CIPD, 2019). Managers hold the key to flexible working – they can be either an enabler or a barrier, and attention must be paid to their role in the process. It is therefore another important step in the operational plan and communication activity.

The CIPD viewpoint is further supported by research from Working Families, who undertake an annual survey into flexible working practices across their membership group. Their 2019 survey found that the most frequently cited barrier to flexibility was lack of line manager skills. Whilst 70 per cent of the survey respondents provide training for line managers on managing flexible working, only 45 per cent make this training compulsory (Working Families, 2019). Considering that their members are already committed to supporting flexible working, we can assume that the figure for other organizations is much lower. Manager training is vital to successful adoption of flexible working, as well as the challenge of ensuring consistency of policy application. Even when flexible working is supported by senior leaders, reluctance towards flexibility or poor application of flexible working will seriously impact the ability for flexible working to thrive.

Many managers are understandably nervous about flexible working arrangements; they may not be clear about their role in applying policy, have concerns about managing flexible workers or how to address issues like workload allocation, performance management or even using the technology that helps enable flexible working. They may not be aware of the benefits, consider that barriers are insurmountable or they may believe some of the myths discussed earlier in this book. Developing relevant training (ideally specific to the organization and its own particular context) can help to address these issues and equip people managers with the tools that they need. The attitude of the manager is critical to achieving the potential benefits, for them, their team and the wider organization.

Manager training must include an explanation of the wider benefits of flexible working as set out above. Whilst perhaps obvious but sometimes overlooked, training can also be a useful time to remind managers that as employees of the organization flexible working opportunities (and their associated benefits) also apply to them! Training should also ideally cover the following:

- The legal framework relating to flexible working and the organizational policy approach where this is enhanced from the statutory minimum.
- An overview of the process, and the specific responsibilities of managers within it, including their decision-making responsibilities.

- How to assess a role for flexibility potential.

- A summary of the different forms of flexible working (see Chapter 1), their benefits and suitability.

- Information on practical issues likely to arise such as trial periods, flexible working requests during recruitment, receiving and dealing with multiple requests and managing rejection of requests.

- Myths of flexible working – where possible, address concerns and myths head on, including providing relevant evidence and statistics. Use the data in Part One to help you.

- Where they can get additional help, information and support – such as HR and guidance documents.

One area that is critical to explore through training is the specific require-ments relating to the management of flexible workers. Many managers rely on forms of day-to-day people management that may not be appropriate or as effective for flexible workers, such as communicating casually when they see a team member, rather than a planned and structured approach. Where managers have team members working different hours or in different loca-tions to them, casual face-to-face contact may naturally be reduced. Similarly, where managers have relied on presence as an indicator of performance, they may need to think differently about how they assess output and objec-tives. Managers are likely therefore to need to adjust their style of manage-ment, particularly around issues such as communication, keeping in touch, 121s, performance appraisal and ensuring employee wellbeing.

Perhaps equally important is supporting managers to assess a role for flexible potential. It is very easy to assume that a particular role cannot be undertaken flexibly, but detailed analysis (usually by way of a framework) may lead to a different conclusion. An example of such a framework is in-cluded in the Toolkit at the back of the book. Assessment of roles must be undertaken in a consistent and unbiased way to ensure that decision-makers do not include inappropriate factors in the decision-making process, or rely on stereotypes about flexible workers.

The more support and guidance managers can receive across each of these areas, the more likely they will be able to practically manage flexible work and flexible workers, and understand its overall broader importance. Training is recommended at the launch of any new strategy or policies, but also on an ongoing basis in order to support new managers. Training can be included as part of existing management and leadership learning and development activities. Wherever possible, have training available from the point of need, so consider including some form of online learning or supporting information to complement face-to-face training.

Tell your managers that the flexible working revolution is coming!

CASE STUDY

Work Anywhere: Public-sector IT department

In 2018, the IT department of a large public-sector organization launched 'Work Anywhere' for around 100 of its IT employees. These employees were identified as holding roles that could benefit from location flexibility, including remote working. Role types included project managers and business analysts, many of whom were already mobile throughout the organizational estate, mixing their time between the building that housed the majority of IT employees and working within the offices of internal customers. Many of them already undertook an element of homeworking, and few needed a permanent desk space. When the office environment was being refurbished, the IT leadership team took the opportunity to improve the utilization of office space and introduce new ways of working fit for a modern IT function.

Those employees who were designated Work Anywhere workers would no longer be provided with a permanent desk space, but would instead use a well-equipped, flexible hot-desk environment designed with collaboration in mind. Employees were empowered to decide where their activities could be best undertaken based on their daily schedule. This could mean working with the wider IT team in the hot-desk space, working in another building with their internal customers or from home.

The idea of moving to location-flexible working was introduced to employees at an early stage in the process, something that IT leaders believe was instrumental in its success. Rather than communicate an already agreed approach, employees were consulted on its development. A small employee team created a set of community guidelines which covered issues such as hot-desk etiquette and ways of working local to the team. This helped to manage expectations and allay any potential concerns about how the new approach would work in practice. The leadership team also committed to taking feedback from Work Anywhere workers a year into the programme to find out what was working – and what was not – and make improvements if necessary. A survey was undertaken, asking employees to share what they felt was working well and where improvements could be made.

At conception, there were a number of potential barriers to effective implementation of the new ways of working identified by employees and managers. Many of these were practical in nature and included issues such as personal storage, appropriate technology and effective management of performance. These concerns were listened to and employees were provided with the tools necessary to enable both remote working and hot-desking. According to the leadership team, many of those initial concerns did not arise when the scheme was rolled out – they were perceptions rather than reality, not unexpected when undertaking significant change.

Also identified as useful to the roll-out process was gaining the buy-in of people managers. A range of targeted communications and guidance, as well as briefing sessions including tips for the effective management of remote workers, were provided to this group. The organization has seen multiple benefits from the introduction of Work Anywhere. As well as better utilization of office space and associated reduced costs, it has helped to attract new external talent, for many of whom flexible working practices were an expectation from a new employer, as well as leading improvements in employee engagement.

Measuring progress and success

Where you are proposing to make significant efforts to improve your approach to flexible working, it will be important to understand if these efforts are making a real difference in your workplace. In Chapter 10 we discussed the importance of collating data prior to policy and procedure development. Such data should also be collated on an ongoing basis in order to assess progress against objectives, as well as identify any problem areas within the organization that need to be addressed or where more focused work is required. This data can also inform future communication and awareness-raising efforts.

Undertake analysis on a regular basis into the following:

- total number of flexible working requests made by employees;
- type of flexibility requested;
- acceptances and rejections of requests;
- reasons for rejection;
- promotion and internal moves – the proportion of which were existing flexible workers;
- overall trend analysis (are requests increasing, decreasing or stable).

These should be analysed by business area or department in order to identify whether there are any problem areas or problematic organizational subcultures, as well as by sex.

Also review employment application data, particularly where roles are advertised as suitable for flexible working. Consider the following:

- Where some roles are advertised as suitable for flexible working, compare this against similar roles that are not.
- Where the organization is promoting flexible working during the recruitment process, review the number of applications both prior to and following adoption of this approach.
- Identify where possible the total number of applicants who indicate they are interested in flexible working during the recruitment and selection process and the extent to which these candidates are successful in their application. Compare this against application/offer data where candidates do not request flexible working.

This quantitative data will provide a range of useful insights which can be complemented by other forms of qualitative feedback from employees. Options for gathering feedback include surveys (specific to flexibility or as part of a wider employee survey), focus groups or 121 discussions with flexible workers, their managers and employee groups such as trade unions where they exist. Six months is a reasonable time frame to allow for those initiatives to begin to take effect and a suitable point in time to begin this analysis.

Consider asking employees some or all of the following:

- To what extent are they aware of the organization's approach to flexible working?
- Have they made use of flexible working, and if so what was their experience of doing so?
- Have they experienced any barriers to asking for or undertaking flexible working?
- To what extent do they feel they could ask for flexible working in their current role?
- How supportive is their immediate manager towards flexible working?
- What is working well about the flexible working initiatives?
- What could be improved?

Combined, these two sets of qualitative and quantitative data should provide sufficient information to assess progress as well as make plans for what else still needs to be done to ensure the effective embedding of flexible working arrangements post initial implementation activity.

In addition to reviewing data about flexible working take-up and the management of requests, consider measuring the overall success of new approaches to flexible working through other metrics. Relevant metrics can include:

- employee turnover/retention;
- recruitment (costs relating to recruitment and application rates);
- productivity rates;
- employee engagement/survey results;
- absence rates (including related to mental health absence specifically).

NEXT STEPS

1   Review the list of items set out in 'the basics' list at the beginning of this chapter and address each of them.

2   Determine your approach for the initial launch of your new approach or strategy.

3   Decide if you want to set up a flexible working network group or champion scheme, or perhaps both. If you decide to set up a champion scheme, determine how these champions can be recruited, trained and supported.

4   Establish your process for measuring progress and success. Set a date for your first review.

5   Agree your approach to training for people managers. This may require a budget in order to either develop your own programme or use external facilitators. This step is an absolute essential. Ideally training should be face to face, as this is a subject that lends itself well to discussion and space for questions. Consider the following: Who will you train? What will you include? Will you deliver this training yourself or will you need to engage specialists to help you?

6   Set up a process for reviewing flexible working application data on a regular basis, ideally every six months.

7   Identify individuals who are already working flexibly who may be willing to share their stories. Depending on the current attitudes to flexible working

in your organization these may or may not be easy to find. Once identified, collect and share their experiences and learnings through a variety of communication channels to make sure that they are available to all groups.

8 Draft your communication and launch plan and agree this with senior leaders.

KEY TAKEAWAYS

- Communication of the organization's approach to flexible working will need to take place on a continuous basis and using multiple channels to ensure that everyone receives the necessary information.

- Targeted communication to and training for managers are essential steps in the implementation of flexible working and their importance should not be underestimated. Training will need to be available on an ongoing basis and from the point of need.

- Organizations need to ensure that all employees (not just flexible workers) have the necessary technology to enable flexible working – and know how to use it.

- Implementation of flexible working initiatives can be supported through a range of mechanisms including flexible working champions or networking groups, as well as sharing success stories and explaining benefits.

- A process for measuring the success and progress of flexible working initiatives should be introduced, using a mix of qualitative and quantitative data.

References

Lyonette, C and Baldauf, B (2019) *Family Friendly Working Policies and Practices: Motivations, influences and impacts for employers*, Government Equalities Office, assets.publishing.service.gov.uk/government/uploads/system/uploads/attachment_data/file/840061/Warwick_Final_Report_1610.pdf (archived at https://perma.cc/5S8P-3T4T)

RSA (2013) *The Flex Factor: Realising the value of flexible working*, www.thersa.org/globalassets/pdfs/blogs/rsa_flex_report_15072013.pdf (archived at https://perma.cc/V4SA-MLMT)

Working Families (2019) *Working Families Announces the UK's Most Family-Friendly Workplaces in 2019*, www.workingfamilies.org.uk/news/working-families-announces-the-uks-most-family-friendly-workplaces-in-2019/ (archived at https://perma.cc/U5HX-UW8R)

12

Conclusions

This book has attempted to make a convincing case that it is now time for a *flexible working revolution*. The evidence case for flexible working is now firmly established. From academic research to industry surveys, the increasing body of evidence shows that flexible working is how people want to work and that this revolution will benefit not just employees but also the organizations for which they work and even have broader benefits for society.

It is time to radically rethink traditional ways of working, many of which were designed for a previous era of work, and move from an approach of compliance with the law to one of culture – a culture where everyone has the ability to work to their potential whether or not they are able or wish to work the *default model of work*.

This book does not, however, seek to suggest that flexible working is a silver bullet solution. Flexible working can present very real challenges; not just those related to practical implementation but fundamental challenges to the very ways in which organizations operate and how employees and managers undertake their day-to-day work. Flexible working has the potential to tackle some of our big workplace problems, but it is no panacea and requires careful implementation to ensure that benefits are realized, and negative consequences are avoided or minimized. Successful implementation of flexible working practices will acknowledge the challenges that flexible working brings with it, and provide business-focused solutions for them.

Adopting new forms of working arrangements presents a fundamental challenge to the way that things are typically done in an organization. For some, this will generate a threat response – a very particular kind of barrier to flexibility (and perhaps most organizational change). Although it is an over-simplification to suggest that all change is problematic, as humans we are hard-wired to prefer the status quo, even when new ideas are accompanied by a convincing evidence base. We like what we know and our cognitive biases are very good at finding convincing explanations that support our existing viewpoints. When we are used to a particular way of being and doing things, it can be difficult to conceive that there is another, perhaps better, way. This can lead to an outright rejection not only of requests for flexible working on an individual basis, but also a rejection of flexible working as a concept.

Flexible working does demand more of the organization itself and its people managers. It redesigns the psychological contact between the parties, and is representative of employees seeking a new deal from work and their working lives. Flexible working is part of a much bigger picture about a changing future of work to which all employers will need to respond or face considerable risk.

Right now, flexible working is available, but all too often only for the lucky few. Sometimes this availability is linked to the perspectives of the individual line manager, particular job types or simply how well-valued or -liked the requesting employee is. Sometimes, it is because a particular, enlightened employer has decided to make a step-change into the future. Flexible working is not yet diffused throughout the labour market, and there are vast differences not only in availability but also in terms of who uses it and why. As we have seen, flexible working still has something of a reputation problem and the issue of flexibility stigma is very real.

Yet those organizations who have embraced flexibility are positive about the benefits it has delivered. Flexible working has the potential to address many of the challenges facing organizations today: how to attract and retain top talent, how to address the gender pay gap, how to support diversity and inclusion, how to do sustainable business, how to motivate and engage. There are some that would go even further than this in the argument for flexible working, identifying its potential to provide us with the opportunity to tackle some of our most pressing problems in society, such as inequality, inclusion and sustainability – assuming of course that it is used in the right way (Chung and van der Lippe, 2018).

Despite this, employees seeking or undertaking flexibility are finding themselves afraid to ask, stigmatized, side-lined, under-valued, stuck or simply excluded from the labour market altogether. Some of these employees are making other choices. Some will simply leave and find a more flexible, forward-thinking employer. Others will choose self-employment or portfolio careers – and it will be the inflexible organization that ultimately loses out.

Although there are organizations doing great things around flexibility, overall progress is decidedly slow. Can a flexible working revolution really take place if we simply wait for the late majority to catch up with the innovators and wake up to the benefits flexibility brings? As well as the growing body of research on flexible working, there are also charities and organizations dedicated to promoting more flexible forms of working. Even then, the journey may still be unacceptably slow. There are steps that the UK government can take to support and encourage flexible working, but there are few signs that they are intending to do so. The flexible working agenda could be advanced through the removal of the 26-week service requirement to make a flexible working request, changes to complementary legislation (such as changes to shared parental leave provision), mandatory reporting requirements (for example, the requirement to report on flexible workers or advertised flexible jobs), introducing a legal right for employees to ask for temporary changes to working hours or part-time workers to increase their hours (Fagan *et al*, 2006), financial incentives for business to reduce the carbon footprint of employee commuting, or the introduction of flexible working by default – the assumption that any job should be available on a flexible basis unless there is a legitimate business reason it cannot be so undertaken. Big problems may require radical solutions, led not just by individuals but also by governments through legislation. Finland provides us with an example of just such a step. In early 2020 they introduced legislation that provides the majority of employees with the right to decide when and where they work for 50 per cent of their working week (World Economic Forum, 2020).

Human resources professionals also have an important role to play: they must rise to the flexible working challenge. It is the role of HR to advise managers on the law and the application of policy and process, but an effective HR professional will do much more than this. They will encourage their organization to be ready for the future of work through providing insight, bringing outside ideas in, sharing good practice and providing constructive challenge. HR has many responsibilities and these vary from organization to organization, but they will typically always include talent, employee engagement, wellbeing and inclusion. This means, therefore, that they include flexible working too.

KEY TAKEAWAYS

- **Flexibility is a spectrum:** There are some organizations that have truly embraced a flexible culture and look forward to a flexible future. They are the innovators and the early adopters. The late majority and the laggards still look on. When flexibility is adopted and approved, a spectrum exists within organizations too, from the occasional part-time role to flexibility for all, and everything in between. Also on a spectrum is the overall acceptance of flexibility; some people see the benefits and others see the problems.

- **Flexibility is not a panacea:** The evidence case for the benefits of flexible working is established and continues to build. Survey after survey indicates that this is not just good for business, but what employees seek. It can help us to solve complex business problems from wellbeing to gender equality. But it brings with it challenges and problems too, and these must be accounted for in any strategy and supporting operational plan.

- **Managers matter – a lot:** In many respects, managers hold the key to the adoption and success of flexible working. On a practical level they decide the outcome of applications, but they also hold the key to acceptance within teams, provide access to technology, or are prepared (or not) to manage differently. Regardless of strategies or senior leader approval, it is with first-line and middle management that flexible working will thrive and survive – or fade away.

- **Flexibility is part of the future of work:** Globalization, increasing availability and capability of technology, changing demographics in the workforce, an increased need for and focus on sustainability – these are some of the key trends influencing work today and in the future. Flexible working is both enabled by these trends and part of the answer to tackling them.

- **Policy matters:** Policy matters, both in terms of what it says as well as how it says it. The language and tone of voice, the decisions made in relation to drafting, its communication and positioning will all contribute to what employees *believe* about flexible working, and how managers and colleagues approach it. Policy not only sets out the organizational approach providing clarity to employees, but is part of providing permission to ask and to do.

- **There is no one best way to do flexibility:** Each organization needs to understand what flexibility means for them, identify their own particular aims and objectives and then tailor their approach accordingly. Flexible working will be influenced by the sector, the role types, the available technology and the work itself. There is no best practice, only best fit. Everything is contextual.

- **Implementing flexibility is a journey:** Introducing flexible working will, for many organizations, amount to a considerable shift in culture and ways of working. Not everyone will want to work flexibly, not everyone will believe in it regardless of the available evidence, and stubborn resistance is, in some cases, likely. Full adoption of flexible working, and the realization of benefits, will take time, persistence and a multitude of approaches.

- **The law is not enough:** The statutory framework is a minimum standard. Following it will ensure that you comply with the law. It will not shift attitudes, realize all potential benefits or change culture. To this, you will need to go beyond what is legally required.

- **Flexible working is not a 'nice to have':** There are some people that will see flexible working as an employee benefit, a fluffy HR activity, something to be tolerated. Flexible working is not just any of these things; flexible working is a serious issue bringing with it serious benefits to individuals, organizations and society.

- **Flexible working requires multiple interventions:** Technology, job design, training, communication, champions, policy, guidance. Enabling flexible working requires consideration to be given to each of these areas and potentially more, depending on the specific organization. No one of these areas alone can affect a culture shift.

Final thoughts

No business can afford to ignore the future of work, and no human resources function can either. No business can afford to ignore trends that are relevant to their employees, customers and stakeholders; to do so invites harm or even extinction. Smart businesses are already embracing the benefits that flexibility can bring, to them, their managers and the people that work for them.

The time for flexible working is now.

The evidence is available. The tools and technology are too.

It is time to bust the myths and drop the stigma.

It is time to go beyond the family-friendly narrative.

It is time to challenge outdated attitudes and stereotypes, and break through barriers.

It is time for a flexible working revolution.

Are you ready?

References

Chung, H and van der Lippe, T (2018) Flexible working, work-life balance and gender equality: Introduction, *Social Indicators Research*, doi.org/10.1007/s11205-018-2025-x (archived at https://perma.cc/78H2-YT94)

Fagan, C, Hegewisch, A and Pillinger, J (2006) *Out of Time: Why Britain needs a new approach to working-time flexibility*, Trades Union Congress, www.researchgate.net/publication/286447808_Out_of_Time_-_why_Britain_needs_a_new_approach_to_working-time_flexibility (archived at https://perma.cc/B87P-XQRV)

World Economic Forum (2020) Finland is taking a radical new approach to flexible working, www.weforum.org/agenda/2019/08/finland-s-doing-something-cool-with-flexible-working/ (archived at https://perma.cc/NLH7-KKZZ)

13

Flexible working toolkit

A key aim for this book was to provide a very practical guide to assist the reader in designing, implementing and evaluating a flexible working strategy for their own organization and its particular context. As discussed in Chapter 9, a flexible working policy is not enough, and neither is a directive from senior leadership. Both employees and managers will need support in implementing flexible working and ensuring that it works for everyone in the employment relationship. Effective, well-communicated guidance documents are one way to complement policy, address myths and enable action. This final chapter and the following appendices are designed to provide useful tools and templates that can support the implementation of flexible working strategies. The range of documents and templates (some of which are suitable for both managers and employees) can be copied or adapted for the specific needs of the organization. Please adapt these documents to suit your own tone of voice, communication channels and particular policy approach.

Written to help managers, employees and HR professionals alike, these documents can support manager training and development, assist in the drafting of policy and other key documentation, as well as provide pragmatic information on the subject of flexible working. These tools and templates are designed to be made available on demand and at the point of need, and can form the basis of a helpful flexible working toolkit. Readers may also need to develop other tools that relate to their specific organizational issues and challenges. Put together in a toolkit style, these documents can provide a clear guide to the overall approach of the organization and what is expected of employees, managers and flexible workers themselves. When considering what else to include in a flexible working toolkit, refer to the chapters on myths (Chapter 6) and barriers (Chapter 7) to identify whether any may arise or be particularly problematic in your organization, and add tools accordingly. For example, if the adoption of technology is likely to be an issue as people in your organization are reluctant to use new forms of technology, consider creating a user guide for online meeting tools like Skype or 'how to' guides for using shared calendars or collaboration spaces such as Slack or an internal social network. Reflect too, on the questions that might arise from managers and employees, and add them to the sample FAQs document. Finally, consider how this guidance and toolkit can be effectively launched in order to support your strategy and operational plan.

Throughout the tools there will be reference to the Flexible Working Policy. This refers to your own organization's policy and procedure.

NEXT STEPS

1   Review the tools set out in Appendices 1 and 2 and consider which of them will be useful for your organization. Also consider if there are any other tools that you may need to develop.

2   Where you already provide manager guidance, undertake a gap analysis to identify what is missing from your toolkit and address these gaps.

3   Adapt the identified tools for your own purposes, taking into account your unique organizational context, and include your organization's branding.

4   Consider how these tools can be launched to people managers and employees, and in particular how they can be made available on demand, at the point of need. Review Chapter 11 for ideas on effective communication.

EPILOGUE

Flexible working post Covid-19

When this book was in the process of being written, very few people had heard of Covid-19. In 2019, around 7 per cent of the UK population worked from home (ONS, 2020a) but by April 2020 this had risen to 48 per cent as a result of government decree (ONS, 2020b). All over the world similar situations occurred; governments ordered the lockdown of societies in order to tackle a global pandemic.

What resulted was a flexible and homeworking experiment on a grand scale, quickly leading to suggestions that the world of work would be changed forever. However, we must be careful not to conflate home and flexible working; homeworking (location flexibility) is just one form of flexible working. Of course, whilst people were working from home many of them were also undertaking schedule or time flexibility. Often as a result of caring responsibilities or attempting to combine this with home-schooling children, many working parents were not working the traditional default model but were working at a range of different days and times in order to juggle competing demands.

For this reason, we must be cautious in the extent to which we use the circumstances of the pandemic to suggest that we are now all flexible workers. Firstly, this homeworking experiment does not apply to those workers so key to keeping society functioning during this time, such as nurses and care-home staff, transport, emergency services, utilities and shop workers. There were also many employees who did not work at all as their industries and professions were simply forced to close. For those that did work, the situation in which they continued to do so was unlike any form of flexible or homeworking in a non-crisis situation. The adoption of flexible working is normally a strategic, planned and organized process; it does not happen in a matter of days without (in some cases) all the necessary tools and technologies. It also does not usually involve working through a lockdown, simultaneous childcare and home-schooling, and the stress and anxiety that will inevitably occur during a crisis such as the one we all experienced during 2020.

However, despite this there are early indications that many employees have embraced homeworking. An early sentiment analysis of social media suggested that employees were positive about their working from home experience (Carroll *et al*, 2020). Research from Liverpool John Moores University undertaken in May 2020 found that nearly two-thirds of employees said that they want to work from home more in the future, with more than a quarter of them wanting to do so more than once a week (Tucker *et al*, 2020). Similar research identified that whilst employees had both negative and positive experiences of homeworking during Covid-19, many of those positive aspects have influenced their attitudes and preferences towards flexible working in the future (Chung *et al*, 2020).

However, and as this book will explore, there has always been a demand for flexible working, but this demand has not in the past equated to an increased provision, even when evidence has strongly suggested it can bring both organizational and individual benefits. We will also consider the myths associated with flexible working and barriers to flexible working adoption and success; some of these have been influenced or challenged to some extent by mass homeworking, but not all. Many issues will remain as we go back to workplaces post Covid-19.

The full implications of working through Covid-19 are not yet known, and only time will really tell if old ways of working have been fundamentally disrupted, or if the gravitational pull of the familiar office environment will prove too strong. Whatever strategy organizations decide to pursue post Covid-19, employees who have not had access to flexible working in the past have now had a taste of just what is possible and how it can benefit them. Where organizations cannot or will not meet the demand, it equally remains to be seen whether this will influence employees' future decisions about the organizations they choose to work for. For those organizations that do choose to embrace a more flexible future, this book will provide the toolkit to enable its implementation.

References

Carroll, F, Mostafa, M and Thorne, S (2020) Working from home: Twitter reveals why we're embracing it, *The Conversation*, theconversation.com/working-from-home-twitter-reveals-why-were-embracing-it-136760 (archived at https://perma.cc/RJ43-SZR4)

Chung, H, Seo, H, Forbes, S and Birkett, H (2020) *Working from Home during the Covid-19 Lockdown: Changing preferences and the future of work*, University of Birmingham/University of Kent

Office for National Statistics (2020a) www.ons.gov.uk/employmentandlabourmarket/peopleinwork/employmentandemployeetypes/articles/coronavirusandhomeworkingintheuklabourmarket/2019 (archived at https://perma.cc/SHJ5-XTJ6)

Office for National Statistics (2020b) www.ons.gov.uk/employmentandlabourmarket/peopleinwork/employmentandemployeetypes/bulletins/coronavirusandhomeworkingintheuk/april2020#coronavirus-and-homeworking-in-the-uk-data (archived at https://perma.cc/WXD4-XX23)

Tucker, M, Wilson, H and Dale, G (2020) The Coronacoaster Effect: Exploring employee experiences of homeworking during coronavirus [unpublished]

APPENDIX 1

Sample tools for managers

TOOL 1.1: ASSESSING A ROLE FOR FLEXIBILITY POTENTIAL

Whether a role is suitable for flexible working will depend on several factors. These can include the duties and responsibilities of the job itself, operational requirements, impact of changes upon colleagues or customers, the amount of collaboration required with other people (and the extent to which it needs to take place in real time), availability of enabling technology, or the need for work to be completed at a specific place or time.

Flexibility can generally take place in **when** work is done, **where** work is done, and **how** and **what** work is done. Reflect upon the work undertaken by the individual requesting flexibility – you may find it helpful to have a copy of their job description.

When work is done

Some roles require work to be undertaken at a particular time, such as opening a shop at set opening hours. Other work can be done at any time – examples might include analysing data, developing a project plan or writing up research. Consider the tasks in the job description and reflect:

- Can the work be undertaken at any time (within reason)? or
- Can the work only be undertaken at a specific time?

Where work is done

Some roles demand that the work is undertaken at a particular location, such as cleaning or providing personal care. Other forms of work will be more flexible and can be done from any location where there are relevant tools and technologies. Consider the tasks in the job description and reflect:

- Can the work be undertaken anywhere (within reason)? or
- Can the work only be undertaken in a specific place?

How and what work is done

Reflect on the nature of the activities of the role. Do they involve working with others, or do they involve thinking, reflection and independent work? Are the tasks routine or transactional? Does the role demand close supervision?

Tasks that involve working and collaborating with others can be further separated into:

- synchronous activities – work undertaken with other people at the same time (for example, taking part in a meeting with colleagues, delivering a presentation); and

- asynchronous activities – work that requires working with others but not necessarily at the same time. An example would be several colleagues working together to produce a report, but each of them can write their parts separately and share their ideas via email or a shared online space.

Consider the collaboration tasks undertaken by the employee:

- How many of them are synchronous?
- How many of them are asynchronous?

Some jobs may involve an element of each of these separate factors. For example, it may include tasks that demand work is done at a particular time but some tasks that are not. A role may also demand some elements of synchronous collaboration and some aspects of collaboration that can be done asynchronously.

Reflect on the duties and responsibilities of the role. Based on the employee's job description and day-to-day activities, consider the following:

- What percentage of the tasks need to take place at a certain location? What percentage could take place elsewhere?

- What percentage of tasks need to take place at a particular time? What percentage of tasks could take place at a time different to 'standard' working hours?

- What is the nature of the work being undertaken? How much of the work requires synchronous or asynchronous collaboration? How much requires independent work or work that requires supervision? How much of the work is routine or standardized?

- Can the different types of tasks be organized in such a way that they can be undertaken together? (For example, can all of the thinking and reflecting tasks be undertaken on the same day?)

If the answers are not easily identifiable, consider asking the employee (where they are in post) to keep a note of the work they undertake each day, as categorized above, over an appropriate time period (at least a couple of weeks) to allow you to analyse this more fully. Ask them to note down their day-to-day tasks as well as when, where and how they take place.

Following this data collection, review the information to identify what patterns have emerged and what form of flexible working would most suit the nature of the work being undertaken (you can refer to Chapter 1 to remind you of the different forms). For example:

- synchronous collaboration tasks may be suitable for flexi-time (as employees will need to work together at the same time), where asynchronous collaboration tasks could be suitable for most forms of flexibility;
- location-independent tasks that can be done at any time of the day or week may be particularly suitable for remote or homeworking (as they will not need to be undertaken at a specific time or place);
- routine tasks or independent work may be suitable for remote or homeworking or part-time/staggered-hours working (as they may only need some interaction with other team members).

Also consider some of the following before making a decision:

- What changes could be made or tried? How could work be organized differently to allow for non-time/location-dependent work to be undertaken at different times or in different places?
- Where work requires collaboration, does this need to be face to face or could other forms of collaboration such as virtual or online engagement work just as well?
- Is the workload realistically achievable in the proposed working pattern?
- Where work requires high levels of concentration, could this be done at different times or in different places?
- What tasks could be split between different individuals (such as through a potential job-share situation) or across different days or hours of the week?

Also consider:

- What are the potential benefits to the individual or organization of the particular form of flexible working requested?
- What are the potential disadvantages to the individual or the organization of flexible working – and how might these be overcome?

- What tools (or access to technology/systems) would be required to support the type of flexible working requested?
- Are there any costs to the organization of the proposed working pattern? This could include costs of recruitment (such as a job-share partner) or purchase of additional IT equipment.
- What are the potential impacts on the work of the rest of the team?

The following should *not* be taken into consideration when determining if a role is suitable for flexible working:

- the reason that the individual is making the request (unless it relates to a disability);
- the seniority of the person making the request;
- whether accepting a request will encourage other employees to make flexible working requests;
- how work has been undertaken in the past;
- the attitudes of other team members to flexible working;
- your personal preferences about where and how people work.

Examples of role assessments

A role that requires both writing and delivering training courses is likely to have a combination of thinking and collaboration activities. The collaboration activities (for example, the delivery of the courses) will usually need to be done face to face and at a specific time and location. The thinking element of the work (the development of the training materials) could be done at any time or location. This could lend itself to a split between home-working and office-based working, or flexible hours on days where there is no training delivery.

A role that requires large amounts of routine administration might have deadlines (such as the completion of reports at certain times of the month) but the tasks do not need to be completed at set times of the day and do not require collaboration with team members, only access to systems, therefore allowing for flexibility with daily or weekly hours, or location.

A role that involves providing college students with face-to-face support will require large amounts of synchronous collaboration activities at certain times of year. When students are not present, the work may change to tasks that are more focused on thinking or transactional tasks (such as planning or writing reports), allowing for different hours or patterns of work at different times of the year.

Where a role involves serving customers in a café, the work will typically require synchronous collaboration, and the work can only be done at a specific time and specific place. Such roles will not be suitable for some forms of flexible working such as remote working or flexi-time. It might, however, be suitable for job-sharing, part-time working or self-rostering.

Where the potential impacts of flexible working are not clear from the initial analysis undertaken, remember that it is possible to agree a trial period of alternative ways of working, without making a contractual change or obligation. A properly conducted trial period should provide evidence as to whether the flexible working arrangement in question was successful or not.

TOOL 1.2: HOW TO MANAGE A FLEXIBLE WORKING REQUEST

Employees may make a flexible working request [when they have been employed by the organization for 26 weeks/at any time] and they may make a request for any reason. Flexible working can take many forms, but usually includes part-time working, homeworking, working at different hours or locations, compressed hours or term-time only working. [See the Flexible Working Policy for more information.]

Managers must consider each request formally and reasonably. On receipt of a request you may decide that you can agree to the request straight away; if this is the case then let the employee know. Also, tell HR if the new pattern is a change to terms and conditions of employment. Otherwise, you should:

- Arrange to have a meeting with the employee making the request to discuss it with them. Try to hold this as quickly as possible.

- Consider the following: What are the potential benefits of the flexible working request? What might any impact of the proposed changes be on colleagues, customers or the organization as a whole? Can any negative impacts be mitigated? How can the request be accommodated? What will you need to put in place to support the particular request?

- Use Tool 1.1 to help you assess the potential for flexibility in relation to the job role.

- Consider whether it is appropriate to undertake a trial of the proposed working arrangements for a short period of time (normally a few months) to identify whether they can work for both you and the employee. If you do this, make sure to check in regularly with the employee and keep relevant notes throughout the trial. At the end of the trial make a decision on the request based on your evidence.

- Explore alternatives to the employee's proposed working patterns if the initial request cannot be accommodated.

- Identify any budget implications of the request or how the work will be covered if necessary. Where there are budget implications (for example, the purchase of equipment) check any internal approval processes that may be required.

- If a request is approved, set clear expectations about how the working arrangements will work in practice. Discuss with the employee how they would like their new working arrangements to be communicated to their colleagues or customers.
- Notify HR of any changes to working hours or patterns. Ensure these are confirmed to the employee in writing where necessary.
- Ensure that you keep records of your discussions or make a note for the employee's personnel file.

In the event that a flexible working request cannot be accommodated, ensure that you advise the employee in writing, clearly setting out why their request is rejected [and setting out the right of appeal]. The Flexible Working Policy provides more detail on this.

TOOL 1.3: HOW TO MANAGE A TRIAL PERIOD

As part of a request for flexible working, employees may ask for (and managers may also propose) a trial period of any requested new working arrangements. As the name suggests, the purpose of a trial period is for both parties to determine if the proposed flexible working arrangements will work in practice. A trial period can be particularly useful when the working pattern has not previously been undertaken or the potential impact is unknown. During a trial period, any changes to working hours or locations are considered to be temporary and are therefore non-contractual.

Before the trial

- Both you and the employee should agree and document the nature of the proposed working arrangements and the duration of the trial.
- A trial period can be as long as is necessary to genuinely assess the impact of the working pattern. This could be as little as a month or in some roles it may be appropriate to trial them over a much longer period.

During the trial

- You and the employee should have regular dialogue about how the trial is working. If any negative impacts are identified these should be discussed as soon as possible – do not wait for the end of the trial. It may be possible to make amendments to the arrangements within the trial to mitigate any impacts or problems.
- Keep records of the impact of the working arrangements, whether positive or negative, as well as your ongoing discussions with the employee.

At the end of the trial

- You should meet with the employee to formally conclude the trial. The meeting should include a discussion about how the trial has worked in practice.
- Assuming that the employee wishes to continue with the flexible working pattern, you will need to decide whether their request is now accepted.

- If you have concluded that the trial period was not a success and therefore the request cannot be accepted, explain this to the employee and confirm your reasons in writing. [The employee may appeal your decision and this is detailed in the policy.] Where appropriate, you may suggest an alternative flexible arrangement – for example, if you felt that the hours worked in the trial were not successful but you feel that other options may be. These can also be the subject of a further trial if you both agree.

- Where a request is accepted, please notify HR if there are any contractual changes resulting from the new working arrangements. These changes will be permanent changes to terms and conditions of employment for the employee.

TOOL 1.4: HOW TO MANAGE A FLEXIBLE WORKING REQUEST REJECTION

Managers must consider any request for flexible working fairly and reasonably, and in line with the time frames set out in the Flexible Working Policy. The entire process must be concluded within three months from receipt of the request [including the appeal]. When it is unclear if a particular request is feasible, a manager may agree a trial period with the member of staff (see Tool 1.3 for more information on managing trial periods). During a trial period, there is no permanent change to terms and conditions.

Where a request cannot be agreed, either at the time of the request or at the end of a trial, you must ensure that there is appropriate communication with the employee concerned. The decision should ideally be communicated face to face, and full reasons as to why the request cannot be agreed must be provided. This meeting must then be followed up in writing [and the individual notified of their right to appeal the decision]. HR should also be notified and copies of any relevant notes sent for the employee's personnel file.

If the request is being rejected after a trial period, clearly explain the results of the trial and why you believe they do not support the temporary arrangements becoming a permanent agreement.

Where a trial period has not been undertaken, consider whether a trial should take place before rejecting the request. If you feel a trial period cannot be undertaken, please ensure that this is also explained to the employee.

Finally, before immediately rejecting a flexible working request, consider whether there are any alternative flexible working patterns that may be acceptable in the circumstances – you are free to discuss any alternative suggestions with the employee making the request.

Remember that a flexible working request can only be refused for one of the following reasons (the applicable reason must be stated to the individual):

- the burden of additional costs;
- a detrimental effect on ability to meet customer demand;
- an inability to reorganize work amongst existing staff or recruit additional staff;

- a detrimental impact on quality or performance;
- insufficiency of work during the periods the employee proposes to work;
- planned structural changes.

Flexible working may also be a reasonable adjustment for staff with a disability. Advice should be taken from HR before rejecting a flexible working request from an employee with a disability who is seeking flexible working as a reasonable adjustment.

TOOL 1.5: HOW TO MANAGE JOB-SHARE ARRANGEMENTS

Job-sharing is an arrangement under which two or more employees share one full-time job. The responsibilities and duties of the job are either equally shared or split, and the hours, pay and benefits of the full-time job are divided in proportion to the hours that each job-sharer works. Job-sharers are in effect, therefore, part-time workers who will have their own individual part-time contract of employment.

A job may be shared in terms of hours (ie by dividing up the total number of hours that need to be worked, with both job-sharers doing the same type of work) or in terms of job duties (by identifying the different elements of the job and allocating separate job duties to each job-sharer).

Job-sharing can help organizations to retain or attract experienced employees, widening the talent pool from which to recruit, as well as minimizing disruption during holiday periods (as the other party will typically provide cover).

Managers should:

- Be open-minded if asked about job-sharing. Undertake an objective analysis of how a role could be shared before making a decision as to whether the role is suitable for sharing.

- Allow job-sharers to have ownership over how the work is shared, and encourage them to document their agreements. You may need to provide advice and support during this stage, or approve any final arrangements made.

- Agree in advance how periods of holiday or sickness absence will be dealt with (for example, are the job-share partners required to provide cover for one another and if so what processes are required?).

- Ensure that there is a written job-share agreement documenting the arrangements for the role sharing.

- Agree how the handover of work from one job-sharer to the other will be managed – for example, will there be any overlap of hours? Agree suitable methods of communication.

- Help the job-sharers to build a strong relationship with each other. If there is no formal overlap of hours, try to find other ways that they can meet and communicate from time to time.

- Treat the job-sharers separately in relation to performance review, feedback and recognition.

- Remember that job-sharing can potentially be suitable for a wide variety of roles, including senior posts. Tool 1.1 may help in determining if a role is suitable for a job-share.

TOOL 1.6: SAMPLE TEXT FOR JOB ADVERTISEMENTS

When including flexibility in job advertisements, organizations can opt to have a standard statement used in all advertising as well as including a job specific statement on a job by job basis. Here are some templates you can adapt for your organization.

Standard statement:

> We encourage and support all forms of flexible working, and many of our current employees work flexibly. We are open to discussing flexible working opportunities with our job applicants. Whilst we cannot guarantee we will be able to accept all requests, we commit to giving them full consideration, and we guarantee that asking about flexibility will not impact your application. Please let us know if you want to discuss flexible opportunities.

Job specific statement

> For this particular vacancy we can consider the following types of flexible working: [insert potential forms of flexible working]. Please specify in your application that you would like to work on a flexible basis and highlight your preferred working pattern.

TOOL 1.7: SAMPLE 'DAY ONE' POLICY CLAUSE

Where the employer wishes to permit flexible working requests from Day One of employment (as opposed to the statutory 26-week qualification period) the following policy clause may be used:

> All employees are legally entitled to make a formal request for flexible working when they have been continuously employed for 26 weeks. It is, however, our policy to consider flexible working requests from all employees for any reason, regardless of length of service. Requests will also be considered from job applicants during the recruitment and selection process. All requests will be reasonably considered.

TOOL 1.8: TIPS FOR MANAGING
FLEXIBLE WORKERS

When you have team members who are working in different locations or at different hours to you, this may require you to adopt a different style of management. Although it is not necessarily more difficult to manage someone who works flexibly, both of you may benefit from you taking a different and more structured approach.

Here are some recommendations that you may wish to consider:

- Set clear goals, actions and objectives for the flexible worker – just as you would for any member of your team – and be clear how you will measure progress against them. If you do not see someone as often as you do a traditional worker, you may not be able to rely on regular observation of performance.

- Use technology for keeping in touch with individuals and for wider team communication. Consider using tools like Skype, Instant Messenger, Lync or Slack. This is especially important for remote workers.

- Should you have multiple flexible workers in your team, consider using shared calendars so that everyone knows where each member of the team is working, and when.

- Ensure that 121 meetings are scheduled regularly, as you may not be able to rely on everyday conversations. Remember that these meetings may need to be longer than more typical 121s if you do not meet face to face on a regular basis.

- Team meetings or events will be even more important than normal to help with team-building and effective relationships. Ensure that team meetings take place on a regular basis – meetings can be a mixture of traditional face-to-face meetings as well as virtual ones. Make sure that information is cascaded promptly and when face-to-face meetings take place always take time to discuss what has been happening since the previous meeting.

- If you have remote or homeworkers in your team, make sure that you contact them on a regular basis to ensure that they are okay and find out whether they need anything from you. Also, keep a regular check on their wellbeing, as you may not be able to rely on observing someone in the workplace.

- Consider whether you need to draw up or communicate local rules or team requirements relating to different forms of working arrangement. For example, if you have team members who often undertake ad hoc remote working, you may want to ask employees to share their locations in their calendar or confirm whether they need to check with you prior to working from home.

- If you have remote or homeworkers, make sure that when they come into a main office location, there is space for them to work effectively. It may be appropriate to set local arrangements about how often you would like someone to come into the office or main location, as this will help to support team working and relationship building.

- If only one or two of your team are working flexibly make sure that you do not forget about them! Ensure that they receive any relevant information that might be shared face to face or in standard working hours with the rest of the team.

- If any performance concerns arise in relation to flexible workers, raise these immediately – do not wait for a formal performance review.

TOOL 1.9: FAQS DOCUMENT

One of my team has asked for the same flexible working arrangement that other members of the team are already undertaking. Do I have to say yes?

No. You are required to consider the request reasonably and fairly based on the current circumstances. There is no need for you to approve a request because others already undertake a similar working pattern. If you do say no, be sure to explain your reasons to the employee concerned.

A job applicant has asked me about opportunities for flexible working in a job interview. How should I respond?

Ask the applicant what sort of flexible working they are seeking. Although you do not need to follow a formal process, it is a good idea to consider whether you can offer any flexibility, as this may open up new pools of talented candidates for your vacancy. You can use the Flexibility Assessment Tool (1.1) to help guide your thinking. If you do not feel that you can offer flexibility, it is good practice to provide the applicant with a reason.

I have a team member who has a disability and has asked to work from home some of the time as they believe this will help them to manage their condition. Do I have to say yes?

Under UK law flexible working may amount to a 'reasonable adjustment' under the Equality Act. Reasonable adjustments are changes made by employers to support employees who have disabilities. You can explore the request with the employee in the same way that you would for any request, but be mindful that a failure to agree to this request could amount to a failure to meet your legal obligations. You can still use a trial period to assess whether a request will work in practice. Whether an adjustment is reasonable will depend on the specific circumstances of the case – you should take advice from HR or occupational health.

I've had an internal job application for a role in my team from a flexible worker. If I appointed the individual, would her flexible working agreement apply?

Not necessarily. Usually, when someone applies for a role they apply on the basis of the advertised working hours and days. However, you may find it helpful to discuss with them what their current working pattern is, if they are seeking this or another pattern, and then assess how this fits with your vacancy. You can use Tool 1.1 to support you in this.

If I agree to a flexible working request, will I have to agree to other similar requests in the future?

No. Your role as a manager is to consider any flexible working requests that you receive in line with the Flexible Working Policy. You may consider each request on its own merits at the time it is received, taking into account the circumstances that apply at the time. If you say yes to one request this does not mean that you have to say yes to any future requests, even if they are the same or similar, as long as you consider it in a fair and reasonable manner.

I've been asked by a team member if they can work flexibly on a short-term basis, and then return to their normal hours of work. Is this allowed under the policy?

You do not necessarily need to ask them to make a formal request if you can agree to this. Informal flexibility of this nature can be part of your ongoing management of your team. Ensure you notify HR if there are any impacts on the employee's salary or other benefits. It is a good idea to agree a date on which the arrangements will come to an end, or when they will be reviewed, and keep a note of this. Make sure that if the employee asks for an extension this is also documented. If the employee wants to continue the amended hours on a longer-term basis, consider asking them to make a formal request.

Should I take the reason someone wants to work flexibly into account when making a decision whether to accept a request?

Generally speaking, no. A decision should be made on the basis of the role and operational requirements. The only exception to this is if the employee has a disability and the flexibility requested may be a reasonable adjustment.

One of my team made a request six months ago for flexible working. We were not able to agree it at the time, but he has now made a second request. Do I need to follow the formal process again?

Normally only one request can be made in any rolling 12-month period. This employee will therefore be eligible to make another request in a further six months. However, if you believe that there are exceptional circumstances you may exercise management discretion and allow him to make another request. It would be good practice to ask why a second request is being made before making your decision.

It is going to be very difficult to assess whether or not a particular flexible working arrangement requested will work in practice. What should I do?

You should consider undertaking a trial period. During a trial there are no formal changes to terms and conditions of employment. The length of a trial can be agreed between you and the employee; what is most important is that it is long enough to give you both time to assess the success of the arrangement. A few months is typical. If the arrangement is not successful at the end of the trial, the individual will revert to their previous contractual working arrangements. If the trial is a success, the working arrangements can be confirmed formally.

An employee has asked for flexible working, but they do not have 26 weeks service. How should I respond?

There is no requirement for you to consider a request if the employee does not have the service requirement. However, it is likely that if you decide not to discuss their request they will make it again in the future. It would be good practice to find out more about their request and why they are making it now before deciding on a course of action. If you feel that it is appropriate, you may exercise your management discretion and consider the request. If you decide not to do so, ensure you let the employee know.

One of my team wants to work from home for one or two days a week. Does this need to be considered as a formal flexible working request?

Where an employee simply wants to work from home on an occasional basis for any reason, this can be an informal agreement between the two of you. However, if this is going to be a permanent and regular arrangement this should normally go through the formal process. If you agree to this request, ensure that the employee is aware of any rules and policies relating to working from home.

I have received two requests for flexible working at the same time. How do I approach this?

Requests should be considered in the order in which you received them. If the first request is approved this may change the context in terms of the second request. There is no requirement on you to make a decision based on the most deserving request; simply consider each request on its own merits in order. You can opt to discuss the various requests with the individuals concerned and see if there are any compromise solutions that would enable everyone to have some element of flexibility and still meet all operational requirements. You can propose alternatives if you wish to do so.

What if I agree to a flexible working request and in the future it is found to be having a negative impact on the organization? Will I be able to make any changes?

Once a request is agreed, it is a permanent change to terms and conditions of employment. This means you do not have the right to require the employee to return to their previous working arrangements. However, as with any employee who does not work flexibly, there is nothing to prevent you having open dialogue with anyone to identify if changes can be made to working patterns to accommodate the needs of the company. If you have any concerns about a flexible working arrangement and whether it will work in practice, consider having a trial period first. This will hopefully prevent this situation from arising.

I cannot agree to a request that has been made for operational reasons – but I think that an alternative may be possible. Can I suggest this or should I only consider the specific request?

You can make alternative suggestions as part of your dialogue with the employee – this would be preferable to turning down a request outright.

What if someone is undertaking flexible working and their performance declines?

There is no evidence to suggest that flexible workers perform less well than anyone else. However, if this does become an issue you can address this through normal performance management processes in the same way that you would address any other issue with an employee without a flexible working arrangement. You can get advice from HR on managing performance issues.

I have received a request but it will not be possible operationally to agree to it without a significant impact on the organization. How should I approach this?

There is no obligation on you to agree to a request that will cause a negative impact on the organization. This is one of the legal grounds for which you can refuse a request. If you are unable to agree to the request then advise the employee and ensure that they are made aware of your reasons. Confirm these in writing afterwards and be sure to make a note of the discussions for the employee's file.

Who should hear an appeal against a decision to reject a flexible working request?

Normally an appeal should be heard by an independent and more senior manager than the person who made the original decision. This person should not have been involved in the initial decision to reject the request.

APPENDIX 2

Sample tools for employees

TOOL 2.1: HOW TO MAKE A SUCCESSFUL FLEXIBLE WORKING REQUEST

If you would like to make a formal application for a flexible working arrangement, here are some areas to consider and tips to help you put together the application:

1   Your application should set out clearly the working pattern that you are requesting, and the date from which you would like it to be effective. State in the letter that you are making a formal flexible working request.

2   The application should be sent to your immediate line manager. You may wish to consider letting them know in advance that you are planning to make an application.

3   If you have more than one pattern of flexible working that could work for you, you can include that in your application. For example, if you would like to work compressed hours but would also consider working part-time if the former could not be agreed, include this information so that your line manager can consider this too.

4   You do not have to say why you want to work flexibly. The right to request flexible working is available to any employee for any reason. If you do feel that it is relevant and want to include a reason you can do so. For example, if you would like to work flexibly because you have a disability it may be useful to explain how the flexible pattern can support you in managing your condition.

5   Consider suggesting a trial period if you would be willing to undertake one. This can benefit both you and your manager, especially if your proposed flexible working arrangement has not been tried before. The length of a trial period can be agreed between you and your manager – it just needs to be long enough to properly assess if the new arrangements will be effective. Where a trial period is agreed, make sure to have regular dialogue with your manager during the period, and keep your own notes about your perceptions of the trial.

6 A flexible working application should include a thorough consideration of the potential implications of the request and how any challenges can be overcome. Provide as much information as possible to allay any potential concerns about the proposed arrangement. For example, how will you keep in touch with colleagues, ensure effective communication and ensure there is no impact upon others as a result of the new working patterns? Where there are benefits to the organization from the proposal (for example, reduced costs) also include these in the application too.

TOOL 2.2: TIPS FOR SUCCESSFUL FLEXIBLE WORKING

If you work flexibly, the following tips can help you to make flexible working a success, as well as to manage your work–life balance effectively:

1 Clearly communicate your working pattern to your colleagues and customers. Block the time out in your calendar and use an auto-signature or out-of-office message to communicate when you are available.

2 If your working pattern includes hours outside of those often considered 'normal' office hours, consider including a note to this effect in your auto-signature with a reminder that a reply is not expected until the recipient's own working times.

3 If your flexible working arrangement includes an element of home-working it is important to establish effective boundaries to avoid work overspilling into your home life. Create a separate space for working if you can, and aim to have a defined start and finish time. Ensure that you take a break during the working day.

4 If you undertake your work at a different schedule or from a different location to your colleagues, be proactive and talk to them about the best ways to keep in touch and stay connected. Let people know how best to contact you when you are not physically in the office.

5 From time to time, build in a review with your manager about your working arrangements to ensure that they are still effective for both of you, and the full benefits of flexibility are being realized.

6 Ensure that you have all of the relevant technology available to you in order for you to undertake your role effectively, particularly if the working pattern includes an element of homeworking. Discuss this with the IT department where appropriate, and seek additional training if required.

7 If you have non-working days, plan for how work should be dealt with in your absence, and in particular about what should happen in the event that a decision needs to be made or a serious problem arises when

you are not at work. Communicate this internally to the people who need to know.

8 Ensure that you are familiar with any organizational policies on health and safety, data protection and IT usage/access to ensure that any remote or homeworking is compliant with relevant requirements.

9 If part of your working pattern involves remote or homeworking, make arrangements for participating remotely in meetings and ensure that you have all the necessary technology available in order to do so. You may also need to help your colleagues to use them too!

10 Never feel guilty about being a flexible worker! Working flexibly does not make you any less committed to your role. Being open about flexible working can help to change culture and encourage others. If you feel that you can, be a flexible working role model and share how you make flexibility a success.

INDEX